T0195709

Cloaked

Living in His Righteousness

ALI DIXON

WESTBOW
PRESS®
A DIVISION OF THOMAS NELSON
& ZONDERVAN

WestBow Press books may be ordered through booksellers or by contacting:

WestBow Press
A Division of Thomas Nelson & Zondervan
1663 Liberty Drive
Bloomington, IN 47403
www.westbowpress.com
1 (866) 928-1240

Scripture taken from the King James Version of the Bible.

ISBN: 978-1-9736-8836-5 (sc)
ISBN: 978-1-9736-8837-2 (hc)
ISBN: 978-1-9736-8838-9 (e)

Library of Congress Control Number: 2020904692

Print information available on the last page.

WestBow Press rev. date: 04/20/2020

Contents

Dedication

I dedicate this book to Jesus, the Author & Finisher of my faith. Without Him I would be nothing.

Acknolwedgments

Always first and foremost, I thank God for the sweet conversations He has had with me, and the education He has given me as I grew in Him through the writing of this devotional. Without His grace I would never have made it this far in life.

To my Dad & Mom, Jerry and Linda Morrow: *"Well done though good and faithful servants!"* Your life-long dedication to Christ has been the witness that not only led me to Christ in the beginning, but also brought me back home when I had taken my inheritance and run away.

To my Children, Jonathan, Peggy & Seth: You are the best blessings God could have ever given to me! For you three, I would give my life, and for you three, I pray daily, that you will find the same relationship with Christ that has so richly blessed my own soul. If I could share with you one thing only in this life, it would be the precious love of Jesus Christ.

To my love, Jack Dixon: What can I say? You gave me confidence in myself to pursue my dream. Without you and your support, this book never would have made it to the publisher. Thank you for believing in me! I love you now and forever!

To my three sisters, Dawne, Deanne & Deborah: growing up so close and with so much love, we have made millions of memories and learned so much through each other. I thank Jesus for the women you have become and pray that I may be as faithful as each of you have become in your walk with Jesus. The love in which you live your lives blesses me every day.

Introduction

I knelt naked, alone on the shower floor, sobbing, unable to bear the weight of my own soul. Tears flowed down the drain with the shower water. I prayed, begged, pleaded for the pain to end. I watched helpless as my life slipped away from me, out of my grasp. I clung to it. I clawed at it; but it just kept slipping away …

Life down the drain …

No more hope …

No more dignity …

Shattered …

I stopped trying to hold on and placed all in the hands of my Heavenly Father …

And He wrapped His cloak around me.

When I came back home to Jesus, I had a long, hard lesson to learn about what it truly meant to have a relationship with Christ. Christian friends showered me with reading materials that should help me to come to know Him on a personal level. That was all fine and good, but I wasn't finding that active relationship that I was starving for in other people's books.

I believe my first *aha* moment began when my church encouraged us to get into *Life Journaling*. At first, I followed the guidelines and read the assigned daily readings while praying and writing down passages that stood out to me, just as instructed. Soon the assigned reading led to following thoughts and ideas across the pages of my Bible as Jesus began to leap off the pages and share concepts that I had never before seen or comprehended, although I had read through the Bible umpteen times.

As time went by, my relationship with God began to bloom. I began to live in excited anticipation of my time with Him. I began to get up early each morning, run downstairs, say, "Good morning, Jesus!" as I filled my coffee cup and then sit down at the table with Him in anticipation of what He had to show me this new morning.

The words I have written in these pages are a few of those *aha* moments dictated by His Voice and put on paper by my pen.

1 – Silence

For God alone, O my soul, wait in silence. (Psalm 52:5 ESV)

Silence sometimes falls like a sweet, gentle, refreshing rain. During those times of silence, I don't have to do anything, be anything, or say anything to just feel the awesomeness of the presence of God in my soul.

But there are also times when waiting in silence feels more like a bottomless pit from which there is no escape. The darkness down there is filled with fear and unanswered questions that threaten my peace. I am lonely in that pit and don't understand what God is doing or where He has gone. I'm tired of being hurt, used, and disappointed. Giving up seems like the easiest way out. My energy is gone, and there seems to be no one who understands the emotional wreck I have become.

I have walked through deafeningly quiet times when I cannot seem to hear from God, no matter how hard I try. Those have been the scariest times in my life. It is invigorating when I can hear His voice speaking clearly to me. I revel in the feeling—almost like the butterflies one feels when one first falls in love. But when that feeling disappears, I feel that my whole world is falling apart.

Over the years, I've found that God is never the one who stops the communication. It is I. I found that my relationship with God is very much like relationships between human beings. As with our earthly relationships when not nurtured, head-over-heels, chocolate and roses turns into work schedules and soccer practice. The newness wears off, and the extraordinary romance you once had fades into the mundane routines of life. It isn't that love has stopped. It's not that conversations have gone flat. It's the business of life that takes over the space that was reserved for Him.

When I rush through my Bible reading and *say a prayer* rather than really pray, how can I expect to hear anything back? It IS like picking up the phone and talking into it when I haven't even hit the call button. In all reality, I'm just going through the motions so much that I fool myself into thinking I am keeping up my end of the conversation. But in all reality, I am too busy with life to pay attention to my own side of the conversation, much less His.

I have seen God's hand in action. I revel in His company, but I am the one who hangs up the phone without even realizing I have done so. My relationship dehydrates, and I begin to live with a vast emptiness inside.

During those exquisite moments of desperation, I realize that anyone or anything that makes me cry out to God can be counted as a blessing. It doesn't really matter what compels us to crave the silence with Him. It only matters that we realize the craving and find the silence we need again.

> I waited patiently for the Lord; and he inclined unto me and heard my cry. He brought me up also out of an horrible pit, out of the miry clay, and set my feet upon a rock, and established my goings. And he hath put a new song in my mouth, even praise unto our God: many shall see it, and fear, and shall trust in the Lord. (Psalm 40:1–3)

I'm sure I will, as a human, fall again into that silent pit. But now that I am aware of the situation, I will make a conscious effort not to cross that border into the desert place.

Now I start each day with a new psalm as I get ready for work. While I am at work, if I am waiting for a file to upload or sitting on hold, I pull up the Bible app on my phone and read or pray.

These sporadic moments throughout my day are like looking forward to a random text message from someone special or seeing that *like* on my Facebook page. They make me happy—these little reminders that He is thinking of me and loving me.

Then at home in the evenings, after everyone has gone to bed, I have my private time with Him. This is when it gets really intimate. No more teasers. Just true, honest, open, heart-bearing conversation in the intimacy of my private space. I am with Him only, and He is with me. I crawl up into my Father's lap, wrap up in His arms, and find healing and restoration in His embrace. I fall in love with Him all over again as He

Ali Dixon

reminds me that His love is unchanging and unconditional. The Father gently reassures my frightened heart that He is not going anywhere and that I can count on Him to be with me no matter what!

For God alone I wait—in silence.

2 - New Year's Resolution

As an avid crochet artist, last year I began my New Year's resolution with a bang. I planned ahead, gathered all of my supplies, set up a Facebook page, and started out with plans to make a gorgeous, crocheted, "temperature blanket," crocheting one row of my blanket per day of the year in the color chosen to correspond with the high temp of that day.

Every evening, as I crawled into bed, I checked the high for that particular day and crocheted a row of color into what would, by December 31, be a beautiful, colorful bedspread.

January went by, and I remained faithful to the plan, posting a picture each evening to the project page along with nearly three hundred other devoted crochet artists.

As we moved into February, my plan began to fail. I ran out of one color and then another, and by Valentine's Day, I had given up altogether because some of the yarn colors I had started with were discontinued and my well-mapped idea was ruined.

As do I, many other people begin the New Year making resolutions to follow a particular plan or to change things in their lives to better themselves. Often, we find that those well-laid plans may last a couple of days, weeks, or even months before some sort of obstacle arises and plans fall apart. There is almost always a good reason or excuse why our resolve ends.

Last year, after my best-laid plans failed, I finally surrendered my time to Jesus. I did a lot of reading and studying in the book of Jeremiah. Throughout those studies, I learned one very important fact about resolutions. We cannot ever follow a plan unless our plan is aligned with God's.

In the book of Jeremiah, we discover that after the people of Israel were taken into captivity, their best-laid plans were shattered because they chose to place other people and pursuits above God. Plainly and simply, when we idealize things, people, or activities, even if they are good things, people, or activities, God will quite often put a screeching halt to our plans to get our attention one way or another. He will detour us until He knows that He has our undivided attention.

> Then shall ye call upon me, and ye shall go and pray unto me, and I will hearken unto you. (Jeremiah 29:12)

Jesus should be our resolution this year and always. When we learn to have a healthy relationship with Him, everything else will fall into place. When we surrender to do His will, the things, people, and activities that He desires for us will align with our path, and we will be complete, lacking nothing.

> For I know the thoughts that I think toward you, saith the Lord, thoughts of peace, and not of evil, to give you an expected end. (Jeremiah 29:11)

Jesus, this year and for the rest of my life, *You* are my resolve. I will let You map out my life. I will spend time in Your Word, listening for Your still, small voice to guide me down the path You choose for me. Help me, Lord, to listen carefully and follow closely.

> And ye shall seek me, and find me, when ye shall search for me with all your heart. And I will be found of you, saith the Lord: and I will turn away your captivity, and I will gather you from all the nations, and from all the places whither I have driven you, saith the Lord; and I will bring you again into the place whence I caused you to be carried away captive. (Jeremiah 29:13–14)

3 - Light in the Darkness

It is interesting to me how God often speaks to us in themes. It causes one to believe that He intends to drive His point in—and deep. Our Christmas Eve service at church was the beginning of the theme that has been popping out to me ever since.

> And the light shineth in darkness; and the darkness comprehended it not. (John 1:5)

Since Christmas Eve, the same message has appeared to me over and over, even popping up in a new, sappy TV show that Jack started us watching yesterday evening. It was only on the screen for a moment, but there it was: the reminder that we must be the light in the darkness.

In order to be the light in the darkness, we must first understand two things: the biblical meaning of darkness and the biblical meaning of light.

The word *darkness,* according to the dictionary, means "the absence of light."

I do not believe that darkness, here in the book of John, necessarily means committing acts of sin. Instead, it describes the absence of God. Awesome, kind, generous, loving people can live in this darkness. Anyone who has rejected God's message (His gift of eternal life through faith in the death, burial, and resurrection of Christ)—no matter how good a person he or she is—lives in darkness and will live in eternal darkness.

I remember as a child, when we lived in Oaxaca, Mexico, one particular field trip that we went on as a group of missionary parents and children. We students shared space in a small school, and that day, we went on an adventure that wound us up in a cave in the side of a mountain.

I remember the fear I felt once we were deep inside the cave. There, in the bowels of the earth, no light existed. Dangerous crevices edged the pathway as we move slowly and carefully through the precarious adventure. At one point, our guide told us to be very still and extinguished the lights we carried with us. The darkness seemed impenetrable. One

Ali Dixon

could not see their own hand in front of their very own eyes. We dared not move, knowing the gaping crevices existed below. There was only heavy breathing, stillness and darkness.

Then one tiny flashlight was turned on, and the whole cave seem to light up. A soft sigh of relief escaped my lips as more lights appeared driving out the darkness and revealing the way out of that cave into the glorious, sunshiny day on the surface of this beautiful earth.

John defined light as *life*.

In him was life; and the life was the light of men. (John 1:4)

Those who walk in darkness do not have eternal life because there are unknown to God. The only way to receive life, is to be known of the light through a personal relationship with Jesus Christ, the Light of the world.

Darkness is present in the absence of light; the absence of eternal life. And darkness is death spiritually. (Wikipedia.com)

In Genesis 1:3, God said, *let there be light*. But the Light existed before creation. And Jesus is that Light before the light of the sun and the moon and the stars. We, on the other hand, are the other lights, the lights that He created to go out and brighten up the darkness of this black, Godless world.

Ye are the light of the world … (Matthew 5:14)

Jesus has given us a job to do. When we accept Him into our hearts and the Holy Spirit begins to live in us, we become the light of the world. Just like when He clothed us in His righteousness, God could only see Jesus from that point forward. God can no longer see us for who we are as humans, only the blood of Jesus. Once the Spirit dwells inside of us, the world sees us by the light that now resides in us. rather than who we used to be.

And he said unto them, Go ye into all the world, and preach the gospel to every creature. (Mark 16:15)

Cloaked

Lord I need the boldness that only You can give me to be Your light in this dark world. I want to shine brightly. I want my life to lead the way into Your light that will never fade. Thank You for guiding me out of the darkness. Thank You for sending the light into my soul. Thank You that darkness is nothing when You are there.

Ali Dixon

4 - My Everything

This morning, for the third day in a row, I started out with every intention of using John 1:1, *"In the beginning was the word ..."* As the basis for my Bible study. But this morning, just like the last two mornings, John 1:1 sent me on a journey throughout Scripture.

Yesterday's passage named God *The Light* and John 1:1 calls Him *The Word*. This led me on a treasure hunt for the names and attributes of Jesus.

In just a few minutes I had a list in front of me of over fifty names; and I'm sure a few more minutes would have produced at least fifty more.

As I pondered the names and attributes, digging into the dusty memory banks of my brain, one name kept popping out. It stood out like a neon sign, a heading to the whole file in which those names are stored ... *I Am* ...

> Jesus said unto them, Verily, verily, I say unto you, Before Abraham was, I am. (John 8:58)

He is!!! He is the light in my life, the air that I breathe, fully man,

> For we have not an high priest which cannot be touched with the feeling of our infirmities; but was in all points tempted like as we are, yet without sin. (Hebrews 4:15)

and yet, fully God!

> For in him dwelleth all the fulness of the Godhead bodily. (Colossians 2:9)

No other name could ever compare to Yours, Jesus. You are everything. You are in all. You are *I Am*!

Thank You, Lord, that there is nothing I can do without, nowhere I can go without You, nothing I can be without You. There is nothing I need more than all that You are - My Everything.

5 - My Great Escape

As I was pondering and listing names and attributes of Jesus, somehow, I wrote down that He is my, *great escape*. But there are truly only a handful of great escapes listed in the Bible. One of them is what I call, *my favorite miracle,* when Jesus simply disappeared from huge crowds that had brought Him out to be stoned.

> But he passing through the midst of them went his way. (Luke 4:30)

> Then took they up stones to cast at him: but Jesus hid himself, and went out of the temple, going through the midst of them, and so passed by. (John 8:59)

Another great escape mentioned in the Bible is the rapture, when Jesus takes home all the believers. The Bible mentions several other escapes such as when Joseph and Mary escaped to Egypt with Jesus to prevent His murder and when David escaped the armies and hid in the cave. The Bible mentions us being hidden in Christ and under the shadow of His wings but the more I thought about Him being my, *great escape* the more I thought, "what am I trying to escape from?"

Jesus placed me here on earth for a purpose and I do not believe that His purpose for me is to run. He placed me here, on this earth, in this very moment, to do a job, to complete a mission for Him.

In Luke 19 we find the parable of the nobleman and the ten servants. The nobleman was going away for a while and gave each of the servants a pound along with the instructions to, *occupy till I come.*

He never told them to run and hide, to, *escape* but to *occupy.* To occupy is to *hold* as in military occupation. Occupation is active. It is fulfilling a mission while on assignment, often in a foreign place, an environment not our own.

In this parable we just talked about, the servants who stayed and did what they were asked to do were rewarded greatly, but the servant who shirked his duty and hid the pound rather than making good use of his time was judged for his choice to escape rather than to occupy.

In Acts sixteen, Paul gives us a great example of how we as Christians are to behave. Paul and Silas were imprisoned, feet in stocks because they had cast a demon out of a woman; and her masters were angry that they could no longer make money from her fortune-telling.

Although they were stripped, beaten, and bound,

> ...at midnight Paul and Silas prayed, and sang praises unto God: and the prisoners heard them. And suddenly there was a great earthquake, so that the foundations of the prison were shaken: and immediately all the doors were opened, and every one's bands were loosed. And the keeper of the prison awaking out of his sleep, and seeing the prison doors open, he drew out his sword, and would have killed himself, supposing that the prisoners had been fled. But Paul cried with a loud voice, saying, Do thyself no harm: for we are all here. (Acts 16:25-28)

Paul and Silas had the opportunity to escape, but instead they chose to stay and occupy the space and time where God has placed them. Because of their willingness to do God's will, the jailer responded,

> "...what must I do to be saved?" (Acts 16:30)

Jesus did not run from the cross but went straight to it, suffering the pain, humiliation and the awful weight of our sins so that we might spend eternity with Him; but *after* our work here on earth is done.

We are called to be over-comers. We are not called to sit around and wait patiently for Jesus' return. We are not called to hide away what God has entrusted us with, but to use our talents, our abilities, our gifts for His purpose. We are called to bring in others for Christ, to be fishers of men.

Lord, I love that You are my shelter, my hiding place, my peace, my rest. But help me not look for an escape from what You have entrusted me with. Help me to not be a feel-good Christian making Christianity all about my own comfort and happiness. I know there will be great joy when I finally arrive home in heaven. But for now, while I am commissioned in Your army, out on Your mission, make me brave. Make me bold. Help me to overcome my desire to just run and hide away in the comfort of Your arms. Help me to take up Your cross and follow Your lead. I am Yours. Do with me as You will.

6 - In the Beginning was the Word

Since the first day of January, I have been trying and trying to use John 1:1 as my jumping off point for my devotional. But every day, that jump landed me way off topic from where I started. Today I began from a different scripture that really touched my heart last night. But when I got nearly all the way through, that message looped right back around to where I tried to begin the year. So here we are at the revelation I was given this morning!

I started out studying about the different ways to minister to different personalities and ended up right back at the *Word*. It all comes back to the Word!

> In the beginning was the Word, and the Word was with God, and the Word was God. (John 1:1)

As I was searching for scripture that pretty much states, "what goes in comes out."

> ...whatsoever entereth in at the mouth goeth into the belly, and is cast out into the draught ... (Matthew 15:17)

I came across nearly one-hundred Bible verses (and I'm sure there are more I did not find) that warn us about the words that come out of our mouths and how they affect people.

Humanity dictates that we answer from the human heart. However, when we take up the old man and allow our own words to come out rather than those that the Spirit wishes for us to speak, we can break relationships and drive people from God.

> But those things which proceed out of the mouth come forth from the heart; (Matthew 15:18)

When we study the Bible faithfully and learn the Word of God (I don't mean just the black and white on the pages, but the Word in person, Jesus) the Spirit has much better opportunity to speak through us. What we put into our hearts and minds is what will come out of our mouths and out through our lifestyles.

> Thy word have I hid in mine heart, that I might not sin against thee. (Psalm 119:11)

> But the Comforter, which is the Holy Ghost, whom the Father will send in my name, he shall teach you all things, and bring all things to your remembrance, whatsoever I have said unto you. (John 14:26)

Lord, I'm counting on Your promise that the Comforter will guide me and lead me to speak only Your Words, not mine. I will saturate myself with Your Word. I fill myself with You, so that when it comes to a time when I have to speak, the Holy Spirit will bring to my mind the words that I should say, and give me the wisdom to know when I should say them. Please take control of my tongue and use me to speak for You.

7 - A Little Lower Than the Angels

As a mother, I have learned how important it is to get down on the level of a child when I wish to get something through to them. Sometimes a parent must get down on their knees to become eyelevel with a child, removing the necessity for the child to have to look up in fear. Sometimes being a parent means getting out the bean jar or a stack of Legos blocks to help a child do math problems or tasting bites of ground up baby food before placing it in the mouth of a child to understand and prepare for the reaction the child might have. Placing oneself in the child's situation, on their level both mentally or physically, always makes it easier to work with a child, easier to understand them and easier for them to comprehend us as adults.

> Forasmuch then as the children are partakers of flesh and blood, he also himself likewise took part of the same; that through death he might destroy him that had the power of death, that is, the devil; And deliver them who through fear of death were all their lifetime subject to bondage. For verily he took not on him the nature of angels; but he took on him the seed of Abraham. Wherefore in all things it behoved him to be made like unto his brethren, that he might be a merciful and faithful high priest in things pertaining to God, to make reconciliation for the sins of the people. For in that he himself hath suffered being tempted, he is able to succour them that are tempted. (Hebrews 2:14-18)

Much the same as human parents must take a few paces back into our own childhood to be understood by our children, Jesus stepped back and put Himself on our level. Jesus chose to come to earth, not as an angel or a king, but as a child, a human child. He chose to place Himself in our shoes, to make Himself very aware of our feelings, our emotions, our temptations. He made Himself like us, to suffer and be tempted as we are, so that He could better understand us and so that we could better comprehend Him.

Lord, thank You for making Yourself a little lower than the angels because You cared so much for me. You wrote Your story on my reading level in hopes that I would be able to digest its content more efficiently. You placed examples in front of me to try and keep me from making so many mistakes on my own. You walked on this earth, led a human life, so that You could feel everything I have to go through. You debased Yourself, took on human flesh so that You could better understand me and be more merciful and faithful to me. Thank You for kneeling down to my level. Thank You for being a good, good Father to me.

I love You.

8 - I Hope in You

> Whatsoever thy hand findeth to do, do it with thy might; for there is no work, nor device, nor knowledge, nor wisdom, in the grave, whither thou goest ... the race is not to the swift, nor the battle to the strong, neither yet bread to the wise, nor yet riches to men of understanding, nor yet favour to men of skill; but time and chance happeneth to them all. (Ecclesiastes 9:10-11)

How do you think young David felt when God asked him to stand and face the mighty giant, nemesis of Israel with only five little stones and one small sling? David understood that even a little stone could take down a giant that had brought fear into the hearts of all the warriors or Israel when the bearer of the stone had confidence in the power of God.

David's defeat of Goliath had nothing to do with knowledge or wisdom, swiftness or strength. His power came from God and in his willingness to obey God. It was in the fact that God told him to do, and he did.

Our faith in God's power to sustain us should not be based on what we think we know about cause and effect. If David had focused on cause and effect, he would have done as all the warriors of Israel had done, turned tail and run, refusing to challenge Goliath. He would have imagined his tiny stone bouncing off the hard head of the giant, the giant laughing in his face, lifting him with one arm from the ground and snapping him in half like a twig. But David didn't think that way.

David's faith, as ours must be, was in the unseen things not fathomable to our earthly brains. Our faith is the substance of things hoped for the evidence of things not seen.

Lord, help me not to live my life looking around at other people and other people's circumstances, trying to find the confidence to have faith in You based on my knowledge of the world around me. Help me to find what You want me to do and to do it with all my might, no matter

Ali Dixon

what the worldly outcome may be for me. Because I hope in You, I know exactly what the outcome will be when I get home to heaven. Because I hope in You, if You ask me to toss a stone at the head of a giant, I will trust You to make it all work out for Your glory.

9 - Your Witness, Your Way

> And Nathanael said unto him, Can there any good thing
> come out of Nazareth? Philip saith unto him, Come and
> see. Jesus saw Nathanael coming to him, and saith of
> him, Behold an Israelite indeed, in whom is no guile!
> Nathanael saith unto him, Whence knowest thou me?
> Jesus answered and said unto him, Before that Philip
> called thee, when thou wast under the fig tree, I saw thee.
> Nathanael answered and saith unto him, Rabbi, thou art
> the Son of God; thou art the King of Israel. (John 1:46-49)

It truly amazes me how different people with different personalities respond differently to Jesus. We see people, like the first few disciples, who just stop what they are doing immediately when introduced to Jesus and follow Christ. And then there are those like Nathaniel who are much more skeptical. It takes more time and effort to get through to that personality type. Therefore, when witnessing to different types of people, we need to realize that there is no cookie-cutter approach. The plan of salvation must be presented in a manner that will reach the individual.

It is a pleasure to speak to someone about Christ when they want to hear it. But it is painful when one must deal with a skeptic on a daily basis. A sceptic will tear apart everything one believes in and beg you to put it back together in front of them without giving you a moment to think or breathe, cutting you off at every word that comes out of your mouth to make another snide remark. A sceptic will break your heart with the stabs and jokes he makes about you and your faith.

> But beware of men: for they will deliver you up to the
> councils, and they will scourge you in their synagogues;
> And ye shall be brought before governors and kings for
> my sake, for a testimony against them and the Gentiles.

Ali Dixon

But when they deliver you up, take no thought how or what ye shall speak: for it shall be given you in that same hour what ye shall speak. For it is not ye that speak, but the Spirit of your Father which speaketh in you. (Matthew 10:17-20)

Our prayer should be that God would put His words in our mouths; that we will not just lash back and speak our minds when we are injured by the flaming darts that a skeptic shoots at us. God promised to put His words into our mouths if we will just let Him.

Now therefore go, and I will be with thy mouth, and teach thee what thou shalt say. (Exodus 4:12)

Then the LORD put forth his hand, and touched my mouth. And the LORD said unto me, Behold, I have put my words in thy mouth. (Jeremiah 1:9)

Lord, help me to be a witness Your way. Help me to not lash out with unkind words when I am poked and prodded. I need Your help. I have a hard time answering when put on the spot, and I've been put on the spot a lot lately. Lord, I don't want my own words to come out when I speak to my sceptics. Help me to guard my tongue and only allow Your Word, Your wisdom to proceed from my lips.

For by thy words thou shalt be justified, and by thy words thou shalt be condemned. (Matthew 12:37)

10 - Presumptuous Sin

This morning I woke up and started my conversation with Jesus. I begged Him to come and join me at the table. I talked to Him but assumed He wasn't listening to me when I didn't hear anything back besides a nagging in my brain to go and fix something I knew I had done wrong. I had left it as it was, presuming that no one would know but me. The nagging wouldn't stop so I lay down my Bible, got up and went and fixed what was bothering me. I return to my chair, picked up my Bible and began to read.

> Keep back thy servant also from presumptuous sins; let them not have dominion over me: then shall I be upright, and I shall be innocent from the great transgression. (Psalms 19:13)

Lord, I was going to use the, *I'm human* excuse. But that doesn't cut it with You. Thank You for forgiving my sins long ago when You died on the cross. Help me to realize that even the smallest of errors is not work well done by Your servant. Help me to dedicate my life to do everything as unto You. Help me not to shirk my duties or try to get by with less than my best.

Thank You for speaking to me even when I do not want to hear what You have to say. A reprimand is communication just as much as the gentle word. It comes from love and Your desire for me to be the best that I can be.

I do not want to do anything with the presumption that You will forgive because You cannot take back Your grace promise. Help me to live my life up to Your expectations. I love You, Jesus, amen.

11 - Righteous

I've noticed over the years that Bible names have great meaning. It mentions in the Bible that Jesus called people different names once they started following Him. It makes me wonder if the names given in the Bible were actually the characters' real, human names or pen names created by God to better get His point across. For instance, *Abigail*, the faithful friend to David who saved him from her cruel husband, means, *My Father Has Made Himself Joyful;* while her husband Nabal's name literally means *Senseless*, or *Stupid*.

I've often wondered, if I were a character in Bible story, what would my name be? Would I be ashamed by the name assigned to me by God, or would I feel His love every time He spoke it?

God has already named us.

> For he hath made him to be sin for us, who knew no sin;
> that we might be made the righteousness of God in him.
> (2 Corinthians 5:21)

Thank You, Jesus, that You have called me, *righteous*. I have done absolutely nothing to deserve Your love, yet You call me Your child, Your beloved. I know I have work to do for You here on earth, but I selfishly want to be by Your side, where I can hear Your voice call my name out loud.

While I am here, help me to live worthy of the names You have called me. Help me to earn a precious name in Your book. Help the world to see me as the person You have made of me rather than the person I was. I love You, Jesus! Amen.

12 – Let Go. Let God!

One of the major discussions my daughter and I have been having is about our testimony and whether or not our friends truly believe. Are we doing enough to bring those who are not yet believers to our Lord? Or are we just living to live, not displaying Jesus in our walk through this life?

We talked about friends who ask questions and then do not listen to our answers or cut us off rudely in mid-response. We read Scripture about how some are called to plant the seed, some are called to water, but only God can grow them.

Reading today in Luke eight, I came across the parable of the sower.

> A sower went out to sow his seed: and as he sowed, some fell by the wayside; and it was trodden down, and the fowls of the air devoured it. And some fell upon a rock; and as soon as it was sprung up, it withered away, because it lacked moisture. And some fell among thorns; and the thorns sprang up with it and choked it. And other fell on good ground, and sprang up, and bear fruit an hundredfold. (Luke 8:5-8)

> And whosoever will not receive you, when ye go out of that city, shake off the very dust from your feet … (Luke 9:5)

Sometimes it is difficult for us to just let go and let God do the rest of the work. We cannot open a flower bud with our finger tips and expect a beautiful, healthy bloom. Sometimes our impatience in letting God grow our seeds can actually cause the seed to shrivel up and die. We can choke out the good work that God is trying to do or even be dragged down ourselves by being too long in the same ground with the thorns when we are trying to help our seeds to grow.

Yes, it is hard to just drop those seeds and wait patiently for God to grow them. But we do need to remember that it isn't in our power to grow things. Let go. Let God!

13 - Hope

...hope that is seen is not hope: for what a man seeth, why doth he yet hope for? But if we hope for that we see not, then do we with patience wait for it. (Romans 8:24-25)

I remember the anticipation of Christmas mornings, sneaking down the stairs ever so quietly to get a glimpse of the magic that happened over Christmas Eve; then tiptoeing back up the stairs to bed and lying there wide awake imagining the treasures we would find inside of those colorfully wrapped packages under the tree whenever Mom would finally come to the bottom of the stair case, beating on her pot with a spoon, releasing us from hope to the joy that was before us.

That is how I picture hope! It may at times be terribly difficult to wait on the will of the Lord. But if we wait, with the faith of a child, the anticipation, the hope of what we know will eventually come to be; it can be just as exciting as finally witnessing the end of the promise.

Lord, help me to wait in anticipation for the fulfillment of Your promises. Keep that childlike sparkle in my eyes knowing that in just a little while I will be able to rip off all that beautiful, colorful hope that has kept my excitement up, and hold in my hands, Your fulfilled promise. Help me to be patient as You prepare the good gifts that are coming to Your child from my good, good Father.

Ali Dixon

14 - Much we need thy tender care

Thou hast also given me the shield of thy salvation: and thy right hand hath holden me up, and thy gentleness hath made me great. (Psalms 18:35)

Over and over we hear of the shield of salvation and the mighty right hand of God that holds us up and gives us victory over the battles we fight. His power, His strength, His might, is amazing and I praise Him for it, and thank Him for fighting for me every day of my life.

But it is His gentleness that makes me great. I am reminded of the old song we used to sing … "Savior like a shepherd lead us. Much we need the tender care …".

Without the grace of God, without His tender mercy, I would have forever been beaten down.

Jesus, thank You for Your tender arms that hold me close to You. Thank You for letting me experience Your gentle spirit and the true love You have for me. Thank You that when this prodigal fell into Your arms, they were wide open to accept me and pull me back closer to You.

You waited for me. And when You saw me coming, You ran to me and washed me and brought me back into Your home and celebrated the return of Your wayward daughter!!!

Today I praise You for Your gentle spirit that abides deep inside of Your strength and power and protection!

15 - Abide

> He that saith he abideth in him ought himself also so to walk, even as he walked. (1 John 2:6)

This scripture really popped out to me today. It made me examine myself, questioning, am I really walking in Christ's footsteps? Am I really living as a Christian should? Am I being a proper example of who He is, enough that my daily life will draw others to Christ? Am I actually abiding in Him? What does it really mean to abide in Him?

When we abide in Christ, we have a connection to Him like the branches to the vine. The vine itself gives life to the branch. Without the connection the branch cannot survive or bear fruit. When we abide in Him, we depend solely on Him for everything. Abiding means to remain, stay, reside or continue. When we abide in Him, we never stop depending on Him no matter how mature we become spiritually. In fact, spiritual maturity teaches us to be united to Him, to depend on Him and to continue in Him, knowing that without Him we can do nothing. When we abide in Him, we cannot help but bear His fruit. It is the nature of the branch to bear fruit and our fruit is derived directly from the lifeline, the vine.

So, the question, "Am I actually abiding in Him?" can easily be answered by looking at the fruits of my life. If I am abiding in Him, my fruit is my witness.

Lord, always help me to remain connected to You. I do not ever want to go off and try and make it on my own. I have no merit without You. I have no root if I am not connected directly to You. I need Your Word to feed me the Bread of Life and I thirst for Your Living Water daily. Thank You for sustaining me. Give me the strength to bear Your fruit and not allow myself to just take nourishment You give and keep it all for myself. Help me to truly abide.

16 - You Chose Me

> When I consider thy heavens, the work of thy fingers, the moon and the stars, which thou hast ordained; What is man, that thou art mindful of him? and the son of man, that thou visitest him? (Psalm 8:3-4)

Lord, I don't know why You chose me. I could never comprehend what You were thinking when You came down from heaven as a baby, lived out a human life here in this cold, cruel world, allowed Yourself to be tortured and killed by Your very own creation.

You have the power to create such intricately detailed galaxies with innumerable variations of life. And yet, You chose us. You picked me. You decided to come here to earth in person and to give up the glories of heaven to visit us and offer up Your own life for us.

There is no way I can ever repay You for choosing me; for forgiving me. All I can do is praise You. I give You my vow that I will live my life for You. I will do my best to make sure that I and those around me are mindful of You every day.

Help me to be bold in sharing all the marvelous things You have done for us.

17 - Good Morning, Jesus!

I woke up, rolled over and sent a, "Good morning!" text to the man I love the moment I became fully conscious; and smiled inside when his message came back across my phone. As I made my bed, I smiled to myself feeling like the luckiest woman on earth for having him in my life. A warm, comfortable feeling flowed through my body, anticipating his arms wrapping around me, his kiss on my lips, the much-valued time we would spend together at the end of a long workweek. Just knowing he cares for me makes me feel complete.

Then it dawned on me. I didn't say, "Good morning!" to Jesus, who was right there in the room with me when I woke up. What Shanda shared in Life Group really touched me deeply. "Jesus sits there in our home always, just waiting for us to say good morning, to carry on a conversation with Him, but we walk on by doing our own thing, minding our own business, ignoring His presence."

What if my relationship with my man was like that? What if I checked off the boxes on a to do list in that relationship? What if I only set aside a specific time of the day to think of him and communicate with him instead of talking to him randomly throughout my day? What if he only came across my mind when the reminder to talk to him popped up on my phone? What if I only spoke to him when I was feeling really good or had a great burden I needed to get off my chest? The relationship we have would have been dead a long time ago. And it would have been my fault for not giving of myself to him; for only focusing on him when I needed him. One-sided relationships just don't work.

> Behold, I stand at the door, and knock: if any man hear
> my voice, and open the door, I will come in to him, and
> will sup with him, and he with me. (Revelations 3:20)

I am not waiting on God's love. I opened the door and now He is with me always. He sits there patiently waiting for me to send Him that

"Good morning!" to feel His love flowing through my heart, to anticipate the time I'll spend with Him. It is up to me now to make the relationship two-sided, to carry on those conversations with Him, to think on Him and love Him with every breath I breathe.

18 - *Patience*

> My brethren, count it all joy when ye fall into divers
> temptations; Knowing this, that the trying of your faith
> worketh patience. (James 1:2-3)

Do you know that feeling when you have a room in the house that
desperately needs attention? It bogs you down. you don't know where to
start. You get distracted by an item that brings back a memory. Then you
realize that you are being drawn away from Your purpose and Your plan.

You stop dilly-dallying, tear the room apart and put it all back
together, clean, fresh and bright. Afterwards, if you are anything like me,
you admire your work for a while. When you do finally walk away, you
wind up back in the doorway at least twenty more times, making mental
statements such as, "Now that's a job well done!" or "You done good!"

I think that's kind of the feeling of this passage talking about joy in
temptation. How are we to *count it joy* when we fall into temptation?
When we are tempted, if we walk into the place that we must go through,
that we know will bring us down if we don't watch out, we must enter it
prayerfully, with determination to change the situation, to make things
right, and follow through in patience; following the path we know God
has placed us on and avoiding caving into the temptation and being
distracted from our purpose.

We will walk through the fire and when we walk through it, holding
the hand of Jesus, we will be able to look back and see nothing, but the
gold refined by the heat. Our joy should be in knowing that in the end
Jesus will say, "Well done, thou good and faithful servant!"

Lord, help me to look to You and the end of the road when I fall into
times of temptation. Help me to keep my eyes focused on what matters,
the finish line, and complete the journey with patience, not allowing
myself to sit down and give up. Help me through the trials and back into
Your joy, Your celebration of a job well done.

Ali Dixon

19 - Begin Again

Have you ever experienced nature in the dawning of a new day? Have you watched the clouds part letting the first morning rays of sunshine burst through spreading warmth and light into all the shadowy places?

The birth of a new day unfolds before you. A coyote bounds through the field looking for his hiding place while mule deer seem to simply fade away into the darkness. The scent of wildflowers blooming and moist earth from the morning dew permeate the air making your heart soar high as the hawks floating above you. As you marvel at the wonders around you, thank God for a new day and another chance to begin again.

> It is of the Lord's mercies that we are not consumed, because his compassions fail not. They are new every morning: great is thy faithfulness. (Lamentations 3:22-23)

20 - His Compassions Fail Not

This morning I was reading in Lamentations and was stricken by the passages in chapter three. In verses 1-17, Jeremiah lashes out at God blaming him for every wrong in his life. "He hath brought me into darkness ... against me He is turned ... My flesh and my skin hath He made old ...," and on and on he goes, complaining about all of the ills that God has brought upon him.

Oh, my goodness! His griping sounded like the old me!

> My strength and my hope is perished from the Lord. (Lamentations 3:18)

But Jeremiah goes on to say at the end of his complaint,

> This I recall to my mind, therefore have I hope. It is of the Lord's mercies that we are not consumed, because his compassions fail not. (Lamentations 3:21-22)

I heard a song on the radio the other day that really got me to thinking.

> ...And what if trials of this life, the rain, the storms, the hardest nights, are your mercies in disguise. (Blessings – Laura Story)

Thank You, Lord, for showing such compassion towards us.

> We have transgressed and have rebelled. (Lamentations 3:42)

Ali Dixon

But still, You have pleaded our cause and redeemed our lives. Help us to look, not on the negativity, the problems that arise day in and day out; but upon Your mercies in disguise. Help us to realize that You do not give us what we deserve, or You would have crushed us, consumed us years ago. Your mercies are because of the blood of Jesus. Help us to realize that no matter what negative we must face; it is nothing compared to the negative we deserve. Thank You for Your tender mercy. Help us to do all we can to be worthy of it.

21 - Jesus, Friend of Sinners

We were having a conversation at work the other day about how some people are so legalistic and judgmental, that they will not even associate with, "sinners," and put down those of us who befriend people outside of our own faith. There was no way this passage could not come up in our conversation and it really sat in my memory for quite some time after we finished talking about it.

> ...why eateth your Master with publicans and sinners? But when Jesus heard that, he said unto them, They that be whole need not a physician, but they that are sick ... I will have mercy, and not sacrifice: for I am not come to call the righteous, but sinners to repentance. (Matthew 9:11-13)

I found it interesting that the people questioning Jesus' actions did not go directly to Jesus about it, but to his disciples. They presumed themselves to be better than Jesus. They did not want to speak directly with God in the flesh because He was a *friend of sinners.*

Lord, help us not presume ourselves to be better than *anyone.*

> For all have sinned and come short of the glory of God. (Romans 3:23)

> There is none righteous, no, not one. (Romans 3:10)

It is Your righteousness alone that covers us and makes us worthy to be looked upon by the Father. Without Your blood, Your mercy, even the best of us would be condemned to an eternity without You. You have made the way for us to live with You forever.

Thank You for sending the Great Physician to heal the wounds of my soul. Thank You for feeding me the Bread of Life and letting me drink of

Ali Dixon

the Fountain of Living Water. You have brought my soul back to life. You have made these dry bones rise up and live again.

Help me to never turn my back on others who have not yet found their way to You. Help me to willingly spend time outside of my comfort zone so that I can show Jesus, through me, to those who need You.

I have been redeemed. Help me to show Your mercy to those who still do not understand even their need for it. Use me, Lord.

22 - Never Alone

…I have loved thee with an everlasting love … (Jeremiah 31:3)

I sit alone in the silence of a sleeping house, drinking my coffee and having a conversation with God. As I read through the pages of my Bible, I came across a passage that took me back a few summers ago, and the tears begin to fall again.

It was a warm June day. I had worked my entire shift at Mission Foods, feeling ill, and getting worse by the minute. At five o'clock in the evening I closed the office and crawled into my car driving myself straight to the hospital, barely able to make out the lines on the road in front of my eyes. By the time I arrived, my world was spinning out of control. I could barely walk. The dizziness was nearly blinding. I was shaking so horribly that I could not even sign my name on the admittance form at the ER desk.

The nurses at the desk rushed me back and they began giving me the, *gold package* of exams, beginning with an EKG, and moving forward from there. As morphine dripped through IV lines, I lay in the hospital bed, heart racing, pain squeezing at my heart and lungs making it difficult to breathe. I lay there alone, feeling for the first time in my life, the total fear of abandonment during my scariest hours. Tears rolled down my cheeks and I prayed for God to just take me home so I would never have to feel so alone again. I was done doing life. It was too scary and overwhelming.

As I lay there broken, I felt a presence in my room, like a warm hug, and heard words whispered in my ear, "I have loved you with an everlasting love!"

Peace came over me and all the passages I had memorized as a child started flooding through my mind.

I have redeemed thee, I have called thee by thy name; thou art mine. When thou passest through the waters, I

Ali Dixon

will be with thee; and through the rivers, they shall not overflow thee: when thou walkest through the fire, thou shalt not be burned; neither shall the flame kindle upon thee … Since thou wast precious in my sight, thou hast been honourable, and I have loved thee. (Isaiah 43:1,2,4)

The tears falling this morning are no longer tears of overwhelming loneliness, but of gratitude for the love I have found in Him; thankfulness for the feeling that no matter what happens in my life, I will never again be alone.

23 - Your Effort Pleases Me

> And I will be found of you, saith the Lord: and I will turn away your captivity, and I will gather you from all the nations, and from all the places whither I have driven you, saith the Lord; and I will bring you again into the place whence I caused you to be carried away captive. (Jeremiah 29:14)

Yesterday morning I woke up a little later than usual, my hair, absolutely ridiculous and in need of a full shampooing to get it under control.

The kitchen was a mess since I had a stomachache the night before and left dinner dishes in the sink. I came downstairs to make my coffee and clean up the kitchen, all the while apologizing to Jesus that I didn't have time to sit down for our usual morning chat over coffee. I explained to Him that I had way too much to get done this morning, and that He'd have to be satisfied with just my prayers as I knocked out my chores.

I finished up the dishes, refilled my coffee and started up the stairs to go shower. I felt a gentle tug at my heart, almost a physical nudge. I felt guilty for putting my best friend on the back burner and recognized His nudge, begging me to make time for Him.

I turned around and headed back to the kitchen where I pulled my Bible and prayer journal out of the cabinet and sat down to read. I opened a devotional, read the starter for the day and began to cry.

> It is the effort that pleases Me-when You keep on seeking Me even though it is difficult ... (Jesus Always – Sarah Young)

Jesus, I am so sorry. I will not back burner You again. I will put You first in my life always. I know how it feels to be alone with no one to talk to. I know how it feels to *not* be alone with no one to talk to. The latter is often harder than the first. Thank You for Your constant compassion, love and forgiveness. Help me live those qualities out in my life, thus communicating Your love to others. Thank You for waking me up and making me alive.

24 - The Power of the Tongue

As I was reading Uninvited by Lysa Terkeurst I was truly moved by finally beginning to understand myself and why I act and react the way I do to life's situations. I tend to take things very personally and feel rejection even when it is simply created in my own mind based on hard things I've suffered in previous years, sometimes quite far back in my life experiences. I have very little self-worth, therefore I project my anxiety and feelings of rejection to people who say or do things that scare me into feeling that terrifying here-we-go-again feeling and I push them out of my life as a defense mechanism to break ties before they choose to break away from me, trying to avoid more hurt by discontinuing relationships before they have a chance to break me.

Today, Proverbs 18:21 took on new meaning. I had a *wow* moment.

> Death and life are in the power of the tongue: and they
> that love it shall eat the fruit thereof. (Proverbs 18:21)

I've never quite grasped what that meant (even though it sounds quite wise and makes for a good quote to post; making me look more intelligent than I am by making others scratch their heads). But that is not what the Bible is all about. It is God's Living Word; put into place to take on new life to each of us as we learn to listen to the whispers coming from its pages.

The second half of verse twenty-one has always perplexed me, so I just skip over it and read the first part only, *"Death and life are in the power of the tongue …"* Simple. Solomon wrote down his wisdom. He was king. He could shout, *"Off with her head!"* at any moment. *"Death and life are in the power of the tongue …"*

But today it didn't mean that anymore. And the second half became very clear as well: " *…they that love it …"* are those who care what I say; my children, my friends and all who chose to do life with me. I matter to those people. Therefore, my words carry weight with them. " ...*they that love it ...*"

"*Shall eat the fruit thereof*" ... those who are paying attention to what we say will consume our words and will either thrive on or be destroyed by them. If I cut down my children and make them to feel worthless, they will believe it and act upon it. What goes in comes out, right? If I build them up and demonstrate to them that they are loved and needed, not only by myself, but by our Creator, they will have much more confidence in themselves and in humanity in general.

The life or death of our relationships is controlled primarily by the words that come out of our mouths. If I tell my man that I love him, he will have no doubt that I want him to be near me and be that permanent part of my life, that second half of me. But if I just stay quiet and never tell him of my love, although I know how I feel about him, he may begin to doubt my feelings for him which may lead to the death of our relationship.

I am so thankful for this new knowledge I am gaining through the sweet whispers of Your voice as I flounder through this crazy thing called life. Thank You, Lord, for feeding me sweet promises of love, grace and forgiveness. Help me to digest Your spoken Word so that the fruits that come from my lips are sweet and life-giving to those who are affected by them.

25 - Until Death Do Us Part

How many weddings have You attended where the words of Ruth 1:16 were quoted?

> ...for whither thou goest I will go, and where thou lodgest, I will lodge: thy people shall be my people, and thy God my God: Where thou diest will I die, and there will I be buried: the Lord do so to me and more also if ought but death part thee and me. (Ruth 1:16)

These words are most definitely a beautiful commitment a promise of love and respect.

But in context those words were not spoken by a wife to her husband; woman-to-man. Those words were spoken woman-to-woman.

These were two women doing life together, brought together by circumstances out of their control. They loved each other dearly and had endured a great deal of love and loss together, side-by-side. This was the relationship of women in a mutual ministry one to another.

This world is hard. We are confronted with constant challenges that women in the past never had to face. Many of us are the breadwinners of our home. The entire responsibility of life and livelihood is upon our shoulders. This often leads to unrest, dissatisfaction, confusion and loss of our own concept of who we are.

As women of God our self-esteem lies in the immense value that God has placed upon us. We are *His* own. But we can so easily forget that. We grasp for that feeling of being enough, but flounder in the feeling that we will never be. We find ourselves feeling empty and alone unable to attain the joy we know is promised to be right there in front of us. Our promised peace seems to be constantly just out of reach.

God created us, as women, to support each other through prayer, encouragement and friendship; and qualified us to minister to each other through our own life experiences. Only women can understand women. We have rejoiced in birth and motherhood, grieved death of friends and loved ones. We have experienced joys and sufferings. We have failed and repented. But in spite of it all we have not allowed life to embitter us towards God.

We have walked with Him, been held by Him and grown closer to Him through it all. We have so much to share. We can support each other with a full understanding of pain and joy. We can lift each other up and help each other to discover that peace again. We can fill the gaps and emptiness in the hearts of each other.

Sometimes our greatest gift can be to lend an ear, to take the time to just stop and pray with one another over a difficult situation. If we love each other and commit ourselves to caring for one another, we can change the world for each other.

God blesses the friendships between women who care for each other completely and sacrificially. The kind of dedication, commitment and support that Naomi and Ruth shared was probably the largest story within the story of Ruth. The Boaz experience was huge, but only a biproduct of the relationship between Naomi and Ruth. Had it not been for their mutual ministry, Boaz and Ruth never would have happened.

I feel so blessed that God has placed in my path, some very special women I can do life with, women I love and respect, women I can fellowship with, "until death do us part."

26 - Frustrating His Grace

> I do not frustrate the grace of God: for if righteousness come by the law, then Christ is dead in vain. (Galatians 2:21)

Frustrating the grace of God could mean using His grace as a license to sin; presuming upon His grace when we are disobedient.

We could also frustrate the grace of God by trying to rely on our own goodness, earn our own righteousness, depend on ourselves to work out our salvation.

Anything that gets in the way of God's grace truly working in our lives frustrates His grace. It is totally illegitimate to add requirements such as good deeds or rituals to the gospel of salvation. We are saved by grace alone, through faith alone, and any inclusion of works conflicts with that grace.

Lord, I know I have frustrated You over and over. Thank You for Your grace so freely given. I thank You that I don't have to do anything to earn Your grace.

Thank You for forgiving all my sins and washing me clean, cloaking me in Your righteousness. Help me to live out my life for You, understanding that nothing I do can separate me from Your love.

Help me to be obedient to Your will. Help me to not use Your grace as a licensed to sin. Help me to follow You out of love for what You have done for me and who You are.

Don't let me ever try and look at myself as awesome. Help me to only see You, like God does, when I look in the mirror.

Your grace is sufficient for me. Thank You!

Ali Dixon

27 - Just a Little More Time

> He spake also this parable; A certain man had a fig tree
> planted in his vineyard; and he came and sought fruit
> thereon, and found none. Then said he unto the dresser
> of his vineyard, Behold, these three years I come seeking
> fruit on this fig tree, and find none: cut it down; why
> cumbereth it the ground? And he answering said unto
> him, Lord, let it alone this year also, till I shall dig about
> it, and dung it: And if it bear fruit, well: and if not, then
> after that thou shalt cut it down. (Luke 13:6-9)

This parable throws me, not in concept, but in its abrupt end that is
seemingly cut short. There doesn't seem to be an answer to this parable
like there is with most of the other ones. But it really all makes sense.

Do you remember the story of Abraham and Lot? God had decided
to destroy Sodom & Gomorrah because of the great sins of the cities.
Abraham begged and pleaded with God for mercy over the city.

> And Abraham drew near, and said, Wilt thou also destroy
> the righteous with the wicked? Peradventure there be
> fifty righteous within the city: wilt thou also destroy and
> not spare the place for the fifty righteous that are therein?
> That be far from thee to do after this manner, to slay the
> righteous with the wicked: and that the righteous should
> be as the wicked, that be far from thee: Shall not the
> Judge of all the earth do right? (Genesis 18:23-25)

And the story goes on from Abraham begging for mercy on the city
if only fifty righteous are found, all the way down to ten righteous. And
God had mercy all the way down to Abraham's request.

I believe that the parable we read from Luke thirteen is the same story, but instead of Abraham pleading on behalf of the people of Sodom & Gomorrah, the dresser of the vineyard is Jesus pleading for just a little more time, just one more soul.

> The Lord is not slack concerning his promise, as some men count slackness; but is longsuffering to us-ward, not willing that any should perish, but that all should come to repentance (2 Peter 3:9)

Lord, I know that all the signs, all the insanity happening in this world point to the last days' prophesies. But I am begging that You do not return just yet. Give us a little more time, time to dig and fertilize, more time to do Your work, time to bring a few more souls back to life. I want to see the people around me come to know You.

I have wasted so much time. I pray for just a little more. I want to be able to share what You have taught me. I believe that new insight, the new perspective that You have shown me, just might stimulate at least one more soul to wake and bear fruit for You.

I believe that Your parable ended so abruptly because You want us to ask for just a little more time. You want us to boldly say, *"Lord, let it alone this year also, till I shall dig about it, and dung it…"* You did not say, "no", to Abraham. And I believe, had he not stopped at begging for ten, You would have allowed him to go all the way down to one and would have still granted his request. Lord do not allow us as Christians to limit ourselves, to just rest in the fact that the signs of the end are here and give up the good work. Help us, like the dresser of the vineyard to always beg for just a little more time with confidence that in doing Your will here on earth, You will not tell us, "no". Help us to be willing to continue the work no matter how tired we may be. Help us to press on, knowing that our mission here is not complete until You say that it is.

Ali Dixon

28 - Occasion to the Enemy

David was the chosen one of Israel, the king, selected by God himself to rule over his people, to be the man who began the royal blood line of Jesus earthly lineage. David was the apple of God's eye. And yet, he did some really stupid stuff.

The first thing David did wrong in this story was to not resist temptation. None of us can prevent temptation, but resisting is required by God. David saw his neighbor's wife and wanted her. So, he called her to himself, cheated on her husband with her and then sent her home pregnant. In order to, "fix," the situation, he sent her husband off to war on the front lines where David knew he would be killed. Then he reported back to Bathsheba that her husband was dead, gave her one night to grieve and then in the morning took her to be his wife.

David was so much on a high about his arrangements working out, that he did not even allow room for his conscience to prick at him. It took a direct message from God through Nathan the prophet to make David realize that what he had done was wrong and to repent. When David repented, God forgave and saved him from death, but not from the consequences of his sin.

> And David said unto Nathan, I have sinned against the Lord. And Nathan said unto David, The Lord also hath put away thy sin; thou shalt not die. Howbeit, because by this deed thou hast given great occasion to the enemies of the Lord to blaspheme, the child also that is born unto thee shall surely die. (2 Samuel 12:13-14)

How often have we contrived or own plans, going so far out of the will of God that we literally have to be given a strong slap-in-the-face, a great wake-up call to realize what we have done and become ashamed?

When we, as known Christians, sin against God; the shame is so much greater than when others do the same. We have a reputation to uphold. We are called by His name. When we mess up, we stock up ammunition against the Lord, for the enemy camp. We provide the means for Satan to shoot at God and His people. We light the very fiery darts that are launched in the direction of our Savior.

Lord, please help me to resist temptation. Please make the Devil flee from me. I know that I can do nothing without You. You are the only one who can keep me grounded; keep my focus on You. Help me to spend so much time in Your Word that I recognize sin as sin the moment it presents. Don't ever allow me to slip. I am relying on You to keep my feet on Your straight and narrow path. I have done enough to shame You. Please help me to never blame You for the consequences I have already brought upon myself. And help me to never again give occasion to the enemies of the Lord to Blaspheme.

29 - He is Become My Salvation

"He is become my salvation!" I found these exact words repeated three times by three different authors this morning while I was chatting with Jesus. I've been considering what those words mean to me. Hasn't Jesus always been my salvation since the moment I accepted Him as my personal savior when I was four years old? Of course, He has.

But I also see it as Jesus becoming the one I have learned to rely on when my world crumbles around me. He's the only one who has been by my side all my life, never disappointed me or let me down, and the only one who has always been there to pick me up when I have fallen.

He didn't just offer me salvation from eternal death when He died for me. He provides a perpetual life ring to get me through here on earth while I wait to get to go home to Him in heaven. Jesus has earned my trust. He has *become* my salvation!

> Behold, God is my salvation; I will trust, and not be afraid: for the Lord Jehovah is my strength and my song; he also **is become my salvation**. (Isaiah 12:2)

> The Lord is my strength and song, and **is become my salvation**. (Psalm 118:14)

> The Lord is my strength and song, and he **is become my salvation**: he is my God, and I will prepare him an habitation; my father's God, and I will exalt him. (Exodus 15:2)

30 - My Portion

The other day I was talking to my baby sister about a little girl in her Sunday School class. My sister was asking prayer for the salvation of this precious, little child. She has been praying for her salvation and teaching her for quite some time now, and just this week, while preparing her Sunday School room for this week's class, she found a note from the child. It read, *"I love Jesus because He is so big and so strong and I want to be saved and be in heaven. And that's why I want to be a Christian."*

Over the course of our conversation my sister mentioned how she is very sad because, although the child is on the verge of acceptance, my sister has to be out of town and will probably not be able to be there to pray with her or experience the joy of leading this child to Christ!

> …neither is he that planteth anything, neither he that watereth; but God that giveth the increase. Now he that planteth and he that watereth are one: and every man shall receive his own reward according to his own labour. (1 Corinthian 3:7-8)

Often, we are used of God to plant or water but are left out of the rest of the journey. We should not allow ourselves to become possessive or jealous of someone else taking over where God asks us to leave off. He has a good reason and a purpose to ask us to pass the baton when He does.

Lord, help me to be content to do the job that You intend for me to do. Please help me to easily hand over the reins when it is time. Help me not to hold on to what is not mine. You have a plan for each of us. If You wish for me to plant the seed and walk away, I will. If You wish me to water the seed that someone else planted, I will. If You simply wish for me to deliver the seed to the field for someone else to plant, or to work hard and remove the rocks from the ground, preparing it for someone else, I will.

Help me to do the portion of the work that You have given to me heartily and happily, knowing that You will finish it perfectly. I look forward to seeing the end of Your good work when I see You in heaven one day.

> But this I say, He which soweth sparingly shall reap also sparingly; and he which soweth bountifully shall reap also bountifully. (2 Corinthians 9:6)

31 - Earthen Vessel, Jar of Clay

All who know me, know that I write for my heart, my daily communications with Jesus, as we share our morning coffee hour.

Sometimes I bare my soul and share my heart aches. But I always make a point to turn them back to praise for what He has done to heal all the pain.

I believe that sharing humanity, being real about who we are, and using our frailty to contrast the mighty power of God, is exactly what the Scripture talks about.

> But we have this treasure in earthen vessels, that the excellency of the power may be of God, and not of us. (2 Corinthians 4:7)

My body and my human life are but earthen vessels, jars of clay I was painstakingly created by God, unique and individual with a purpose in mind; fearfully and wonderfully designed, functional for His purpose. This body is a temporary housing for a permanent treasure. The miracle is that Jesus chose this jar of clay, with all its chips and flaws, to fill with His great treasure, and personal relationship with Him.

Lord, use my plain, earthiness to really show off the power of You. Let people see the huge contrast in the vessel that I am and the treasure that flows from me. Let the contrast be witness that makes men see the strength, and power, and joy that flow from me are not my own but only by Your strengthening grace. Thank You for choosing and using me.

Ali Dixon

32 - Treasures in Heaven

> Ye have not chosen me, but I have chosen you, and ordained you, that ye should go and bring forth fruit, and that your fruit should remain: that whatsoever ye shall ask of the Father in my name, he may give it you. (John 15:16)

This passage perfectly explains the discussion we were having at work the other day. A coworker and I were talking about our mission, our purpose here on earth. We discussed how feel-good Christianity seems to be taking over the planet and people are falling away from Christ because of it. No one wants to do the work that we are ordained to do. No one wants to bring forth fruit. All we want to do is collect, *"ask and ye shall receive."*

But those who preach this kind of gospel are only preaching half of the truth, half of the gospel, half of the Christian life.

> Beware of false prophets, which come to you in sheep's clothing, but inwardly they are ravening wolves. (Matthew 7:15)

If we are not careful, we fall into the trap thinking that we must do nothing but sit back and enjoy the fruits of Jesus' work rather than our own. We want to sit back and watch Him carry that cross to Calvary and rejoice in the grace and mercy He bestowed on us through His death, burial and resurrection. But we don't want to pick up a cross and follow.

Feel-good Christianity teaches that the Gift of God is not just eternal life, but happiness riches here on earth. *False!* Those things are only promised in heaven *if* we do the job Christ called us to do here on earth.

> Not every one that saith unto me, Lord, Lord, shall enter
> into the kingdom of heaven; but he that doeth the will of
> my Father which is in heaven. (Matthew 7:21)

Lord, help us to realize that Christianity is not about us. Help us to not follow the false doctrine that God will make our life here on earth happy-go-lucky. Help us to dedicate to doing the job You ordained us to do. Help us to do our work heartily as unto You. Help us to do Your will always and be prepared to not receive the rewards You promised while we are here on earth. Let us do what You need done out of love for You for what You have already done.

> Lay not up for yourselves treasures upon earth, where
> moth and rust doth corrupt, and where thieves break
> through and steal: But lay up for yourselves treasures
> in heaven … For where your treasure is, there will your
> heart be also. (Matthew 6:19-21)

33 - Companion of Fools

He that walketh with wise men shall be wise: but a companion of fools shall be destroyed. (Proverbs 13:20)

When my children were still in youth group, Pastor Nate did a visual demonstration for the students to help them comprehend this passage. He had one student stand on a chair and one on the floor at his feet. He asked the students to hold each other's hands and pull on each other. The student on the chair was to attempt to pull the student on the floor up and the student on the floor was to attempt to pull the student on the chair down.

When the student on the floor pulled the student from the chair, Pastor Nate was able to show by the object lesson, that it is easier to pull someone down than to lift them up.

We talked a while back about Jesus being a friend of sinners. But just because He was, *a friend of tax collectors and sinners*, it doesn't mean that He winked at sin. He was only a "friend of sinners" in the fact that He welcomed those sinners who were of a contrite spirit, open to the gospel, truly repentant and on the road to putting their faith in Him.

Jesus allowed a sinful woman to anoint His feet when everyone else wanted to send her away. When the people rebuked Him for associating with her, He said,

Her sins, which are many, are forgiven; for she loved much … (Luke 7:47)

Jesus sat with the tax collectors when He was seeking out His disciple, Matthew. When the Pharisees reprimanded Him for associating with the likes He said,

They that be whole need not a physician, but they that are sick. But go ye and learn what that meaneth, I will have mercy, and not sacrifice: for I am not come to call the righteous, but sinners to repentance. (Matthew 9:12-13)

Lord, while we are about Your business, do not allow us to slip into the trap that associating with sinners just to associate is ok. Help us to be kind and loving to all, but not fall into the path they are on. Help us to only go where You lead and keep a keen eye open for the fiery darts of the Devil while we are out of Your element. Guard our hearts and keep us clean. Help us to stand out when we are among those who do not believe. Help our witness and our testimony draw people to You. Help us to not use Your association with sinners as our license to stay where we do not belong. Help us not to believe ourselves to be stronger than the sin around us. Help us to always be aware that it is easier to fall than to pull someone up.

Be not overcome of evil, but overcome evil with good. (Romans 12:21)

34 - Back Eyes

When my children were young, and I would catch them doing something they were not supposed to do; they would ask how I knew what they were doing. I always teased and said, "I'm a mom. All moms have eyes in the back of their heads." One evening, Seth stood behind me on the couch, playing with my hair as was his norm when he was little. Rather than brushing it and putting it in funny styles, this time he seemed to be digging through my hair looking for something in my scalp. It was a bit uncomfortable, so I asked him what he was doing. He piped back very quickly, "Mom, I'm looking for your back eyes!"

> Therefore whatsoever ye have spoken in darkness shall
> be heard in the light; and that which ye have spoken in
> the ear in closets shall be proclaimed upon the housetops.
> (Luke 12:3)

God's relationship with us is very much like a parent/child relationship. He sees all.

I've always taught my children that they should never put up anything on social media or send anything in emails, texts, etc. that they would be ashamed to share with Jesus. He walks beside us every step of our day. The Holy Spirit inside of us goes everywhere we go and is subjected to every environment and activity that we subject ourselves to.

Lord, help us to be keenly aware of Your presence. Help us to live our lives for Your glory. Help us to understand, that although You may not shout our wrongdoings from the housetops, Satan is constantly looking for anything he can use against us as Christians to smear our name and Your name along with it. Help us to focus our minds on You. Help us to live our lives for Your glory and not our own.

35 - Migraine Cocktail

Living with migraines was a routine of my life. No one could understand how I could function the way I did, "if I was really in all that pain."

But similar to a three-legged dog who can run and play with the rest of the pack; over time, our deficiencies become a part of who we are. We learn to live with them, accepting them as a routine part of life, and coping because we must.

After I started seeing Dr. Thomas and taking his "migraine cocktail" (a bunch of vitamins specifically combined for the relief of migraines) on a regular basis, my migraines have been drastically reduced to the point that they are no longer a daily challenge. Now, when I do get them, the pain is nearly unbearable because it is now out of the ordinary, no longer a normal part of my life.

Just like these migraines, anything can become common, a routine, ordinary part of any life. Shameful things become standard and soon don't even seem out of place.

Our world has become saturated with "routine migraines." Terrible things are happening all around us, and society shrugs them off as, "just another thing." Our society has become so depraved that it is called, "normal," for innocent babies to be killed before they exit the womb. Rampant perversion, the loss of values and morality, complete social breakdown is everywhere around us.

When a nation turns its back on God it becomes depraved. Sin becomes "normal." Condoning sin impedes our ability to hate it, to feel the pain. We as a nation need to be medicated. We need to saturate ourselves with the Word of God, our moral, migraine cocktail, so that sin stands out and is painful. It needs to get our attention and let us know when something is wrong.

However bleak and impossible it may seem, there is hope. Do you remember the story of Jonah and how the stench of Nineveh's sin went

Ali Dixon

up to God's nose? God sent Jonah to Nineveh to demand that they turn away from their depravity. And they listened. There is hope!

Lord, we, as a nation, need You as our physician, to give us what we need for healing. We need to be able to feel the pain of sin. We need to not just sweep sin under the rug and call it normal.

Help us as Christians to be brave enough to let our candles shine brightly and be different for You. Help us to help people understand that sin is not normal. Help us as a nation to come back home to You. Please fix the moral compass of society. Help us to feel the good days so much that our migraine days hurt bad.

Do what You can to bring this once great nation back to You. Make it hurt if You must. But bring us home. I promise to do my part, to bear my portion of the weight of sharing Your medicine with this deprived society.

Blessed be the nation whose God is the Lord.

> And Jesus answering said unto them, They that are whole need not a physician; but they that are sick. I came not to call the righteous, but sinners to repentance. (Luke 5:31-32)

36 - Purpose

Jack bought me a robotic vacuum to help me out around the house. That vacuum has but one purpose, to roll through the house picking up dirt and dog hair so that when I go to do my cleaning, there is much less for me to do. When that vacuum gets stuck in a corner and cannot get out, it literally screams at me, beeping and flashing a red light letting me know something is wrong. Once I free it from where it is stuck and allow it to do its job again, the light goes green and it goes about its merry way as though nothing were wrong in its own little world. This little robot is smart, and slowly is teaching itself the layout of the house, learning where not to go to avoid getting stuck in those problem corners.

One thing that I have learned through it all is that when we are at our lowest, heaviest moments, the best way to bring ourselves up out of the dumps is to do something for someone else. The joy in giving of ourselves can lift us up from, "the depths of despair."

Why is that? Well, didn't God give us the commandment to love one another? Isn't our purpose to serve? When we are focused on our own problems, we are not doing what we were created to do. We are not performing our duty as we were designed.

> Master, which is the great commandment in the law? Jesus said unto him, Thou shalt love the Lord thy God with all thy heart, and with all thy soul, and with all thy mind. This is the first and great commandment. And the second is like unto it, Thou shalt love thy neighbour as thyself. On these two commandments hang all the law and the prophets. (Matthew 22:36-40)

Lord, help us to learn those trouble corners in our lives that will trap us and bring us down, hindering us from doing what we were designed to do. Help us to focus on the path You have prepared for us, and to happily perform the purpose You have called us to.

Ali Dixon

37 - Be Ye Separate

> Having therefore these promises, dearly beloved, let us cleanse ourselves from all filthiness of the flesh and spirit, perfecting holiness in the fear of God. (2 Corinthians 7:1)

Lately I've been doing a lot of thinking about the promises of God that so many Christians tout while leaving out the part where we put in the work to earn the reward. I was reading 2 Corinthians seven this morning and had to go back to chapter six to find out what promises this passage was talking about.

> Wherefore come out from among them, and be ye separate, saith the Lord, and touch not the unclean thing; and I will receive you, And will be a Father unto you, and ye shall be my sons and daughters, saith the Lord Almighty. (2 Corinthians6 :17-18)

The passages brought me right back to, *be ye separate*. I started this year finding the theme about being the light of the world everywhere. And now, not that far into the year, the theme seems to have forked off from being the light, to being separate, uniquely different from the world.

Lord, thank You for promising to be my Father. Thank You for giving me the opportunity to be born again, a citizen of heaven, a child of the King. Help me to be bold in separating myself from the old self and show the world that I am Yours and You are mine. Help me to remember that my home is not here on earth. Help me to always remember the promise that You have a place waiting for me in heaven when my work here on earth is done.

I so look forward to joining You, my Father, at home.

38 - Comfort Zones

Comfort zones are nice. Goals and plans and dreams put that feel-good, contentment inside of us. We feel large and in charge when the world is going our way and we feel a sense of mastery over our own lives. But control is an illusion.

> Go to now, ye that say, To day or to morrow we will go into such a city, and continue there a year, and buy and sell, and get gain: Whereas ye know not what shall be on the morrow. For what is your life? It is even a vapour, that appeareth for a little time, and then vanisheth away. (James 4:13-14)

God chose the path for our lives long before we were ever born. Along those paths we go through seasons; seasons of great joy, seasons of sorrow and mourning, and seasons of strict contentment.

Just because we come upon a season in our lives were things change and good things crumble, it doesn't mean that we have done anything wrong. It simply means that the seasons are changing, and God's purpose is about to take on a new look.

Sunshine may turn to snow, but we must look for the beauty in the new season. Look for the magic, the newness, not the cold and the frost. Our lives are like a vapor. Because they vanish so quickly, He must pack in His purpose into a very short space in time.

Lord, help me to be excited over the change of seasons in my life. Going from the warmth of summertime can be hard when we step directly into the cold harshness of winter. Stay by my side. Guide me and lead me. Don't let my feet slide out from under me on the icy ground. Wrap me in the warmth of Your love and grace. Fill me with Your Spirit so that I feel Your warmth from the inside out. Help me along the way. Guide my feet when I cannot see the path for the snow. And stay with me into the next season when the snow will again melt away, new buds will appear on the trees, and life, once again will feel right.

Your ways are always better than my ways. Help me to trust You Jesus.

39 - You Are My Defense

> For we wrestle not against flesh and blood, but against principalities, against powers, against the rulers of the darkness of this world, against spiritual wickedness in high places. (Ephesians 6:12)

Over the years I have learned that the Christian life is not all a beautiful, joyful happy dance. It isn't a life of luxury as many false teachers would lead us to believe. Casting our bread on the waters isn't talking about financial or physical gain.

When we truly start walking with Jesus, that is when we find out just how alive and real the devil truly is. Many believers are surprised to find out that the Christian life is one of intense opposition, most of it spiritual.

Satan has some really sneaky weapons that he loves to use on us to try and cause us to fall and to fail in our battle with him. First of all, Satan is a deceiver. He mixes up the truth and tries to confuse us into believing a lie. If we are not careful to stay in the Scripture and truly know it, we can be misled by similar doctrines that can lead us down paths that God did not lay out for us. Satan's deception is what brought mankind into sin in the garden of Eden.

Satan can cause us to question the very existence of God. When we see so many things that go wrong in this world, we can begin to wonder if God is real and alive. If we do not stay in God's Word and in constant communication with Him, we will begin to feel lonely and start to doubt His authority and then His existence.

Satan loves to work through depression and depression can be contagious. I honestly believe that this is the weapon that Satan prefers to use against me personally. When I feel like I am truly becoming closer to God, Satan likes to bring up my past and tries to drag me down, reminding me how unworthy I am of Christ. Those feelings of hopelessness and discouragement sadden the heart and cause us to lose our spirit, our strength.

Ali Dixon

There are so many other spiritual weapons that Satan can and will use against the Christian who is seeking after God. He seems to understand which weapon will be the most effective on which believer. He then wields that weapon against us doesn't let up.

But God has given us a powerful armory in defense of Satan. If we learn to simply pick up the tools provided and use them as instructed, we can defend from the fiery darts of the Devil.

> Put on the whole armour of God, that ye may be able to stand against the wiles of the devil. For we wrestle not against flesh and blood, but against principalities, against powers, against the rulers of the darkness of this world, against spiritual wickedness in high places. Wherefore take unto you the whole armour of God, that ye may be able to withstand in the evil day, and having done all, to stand. Stand therefore, having your loins girt about with truth, and having on the breastplate of righteousness; And your feet shod with the preparation of the gospel of peace; Above all, taking the shield of faith, wherewith ye shall be able to quench all the fiery darts of the wicked. And take the helmet of salvation, and the sword of the Spirit, which is the word of God: Praying always with all prayer and supplication in the Spirit, and watching thereunto with all perseverance and supplication for all saints; (Ephesians 6:11-18)

Lord, You are my defense. When You are with me, nothing can stand against. When it comes to fighting the spiritual battle with Satan, please keep me in perfect peace because my mind is stayed on You. Help me to be anxious for nothing, but in everything by prayer and supplication with thanksgiving, let my requests be made known to You. Help me to stand victorious against the rulers of the darkness of this world. I can only do this through You.

40 - Wages vs. Gift

I recently had a conversation with a coworker who is nearing retirement. She was talking about her dilemma in trying to decide if she is to go on working or to quit and stay at home. Upon her birthday this year, she will begin to take in half of her husband's retirement pay from the railroad. It was part of his benefits packet, and, would be a greater income than what she currently earns working in the insurance office with me. If she continues working, she must declare any income she receives, and her retirement pay from the railroad is reduced dollar-for dollar by what she is earning as income elsewhere.

I didn't see it as a dilemma at all. Why would one continue working when they could bring in the same amount of money staying at home? What I wouldn't give to be able to spend my entire day in my home, making it sparkly for my family and having more time to spend with God ... not to mention having more time for outdoor adventures like fishing, hunting, kayaking and hiking. To me, the decision would be a no-brainer.

> For the wages of sin is death; but the gift of God is eternal
> life through Jesus Christ our Lord. (Romans 6:23)

So why is it so difficult for the human race to decide between wages and a free gift? Especially when the wage of sin is death and the free gift of God is eternal life. I just don't get it. No dilemma here.

But somehow, we as humans, tend to be afraid of the gift. Maybe it's skepticism. "Nothing comes free" is what we've always been taught. Why would Jesus lay down His life of His own free will and take our sins to hell when He was perfect and without sin? It really doesn't make sense.

But Jesus is God and was in the beginning with God when He created mankind. He formed us from the dust of the ground, but in His image. We were His creation, His masterpiece. He breathed His own breath into us and gave us life in the beginning. When man turned from Him and chose sin, His heart was broken. He had to do everything in His power to win us back. Because of this great, unconditional love, He gave his life for us. He died a cruel death on the cross, took our sins and buried them in hell, then rose again so that He could be with us always.

Lord, use me to encourage people to choose Your gift of eternal life over the wages of sin, eternal death. Help me to show them that the gift is real and unconditional. Help my life to demonstrate the joy of living for You rather than working myself to death. Thank You for Your gift of eternal life. I can't wait to begin my retirement by Your side, forever in heaven with You.

41 - The Secret Place

I've been thinking a lot about the "secret place" mentioned in Psalm 91:1. The more I ponder it, the more excited I get. My mind wanders back to excerpts from, "The Secret Garden".

> She put her hands under the leaves and began to pull and push them aside. Thick as the ivy hung, it nearly all was a loose and swinging curtain, though some had crept over wood and iron. Mary's heart began to thump and her hands to shake a little in her delight and excitement. The robin kept singing and twittering away and tilting his head on one side, as if he were as excited as she was. What was this under her hands which was square and made of iron and which her fingers found a hole in?

> It was the lock of the door which had been closed ten years and she put her hand in her pocket, drew out the key and found it fitted the keyhole. She put the key in and turned it. It took two hands to do it, but it did turn.

> And then she took a long breath and looked behind her up the long walk to see if any one was coming. No one was coming. No one ever did come, it seemed, and she took another long breath, because she could not help it, and she held back the swinging curtain of ivy and pushed back the door which opened slowly ... slowly.

> Then she slipped through it, and shut it behind her, and stood with her back against it, looking about her and breathing quite fast with excitement, and wonder, and delight.

Ali Dixon

She was standing inside the secret garden ... (The Secret
Garden – Frances Hodgson Burnett)

I accepted Christ into my heart at a very young age. I know that He
saved me and that there is no possibility of me going anywhere but heaven
when I die because He promised that my salvation is permanent, a second
birth, something that could never be undone, no matter what. I believed
that with my whole heart. And maybe that strong faith in my eternal
salvation was the beginning of my problem. Sounds strange, right?

After I received Christ I just went on with my life as usual. But, really,
what changes could have been expected in my four-year-old life? I grew
up in a Christian home where we spent every evening gathered together
for family devotions. We went to church at least three times per week.
My parents were called to the mission field when I was only four. We
moved into deep southern Mexico when I was only eight. I was home or
private schooled all my life, and pretty much sheltered from any outside
influences that would have allowed my salvation to be witnessed on a
large scale as it would have been if I had found Him in my adulthood.

As I grew older, the lack of outside influences developed my love for
reading. I loved to read so much that when I messed up, my mother could
find no better punishment than to ground me from my best friends in
the world, my books.

We lived on a very meager independent missionary income which
left little money to invest in new reading materials every time I finished
another book. So, I read and re-read the same novels over and over until
the pages nearly fell out of their bindings. There wasn't a Zane Grey,
Louis L'amour or Grace Livingston Hill character that I didn't know as
well as my own sisters, if not better. And though I loved so dearly to read,
my parents had to force me to read my daily devotions. It was a chore to
have to sit and read those same old passages again and again. I had heard
them time and again since the day I was born and was nowhere near as
intrigued by them as I was by the old west adventures of the Sackets!

And prayer ... "Thank You, Jesus for this day. Help me to sleep well
and not have any bad dreams. Take care of everyone I love. Amen." Wow!
Those were deep conversations with the One who had promised me
eternal life. My poor Father must have felt so lonely for me as He watched

me drift farther and farther away from Him, off into my own little world where nothing was as important to me as what was important to me.

As I grew into an adult, my life really began to deviate from the path God had mapped out for me before I was ever born. Romantic relationships never worked out well for me. I settled over and over for men who were not of God's choosing. Every one of those relationships ended in disaster. I didn't believe myself worthy of anything better than the outcome I was receiving. But I made excuses for my misery. I blamed God for all my heartbreak, mourning and the hurt I was going through. I shook my fist in His face. "If You were the loving Father You claim to be, why do You allow all of this pain and abuse in Your daughter's life? I drifted farther and farther away from Him and allowed myself to simply survive. By then I had totally forgotten that God's promises are not handouts, but rewards for those who diligently seek Him.

Fast-forward three live births and a few years later ...

In October of 2013 I moved my family to Colorado to better myself financially with my company. I didn't ask my family about the move, much less God. I just looked at the dollar amount and accepted the promotion. Little did I know the road that would put us on.

My youngest son was twelve years old at the time and became so depressed with the move, loss of friends and the bullying at his new school; that he began to withdraw from the family and then from life itself. After school he would go in his room and curl up in a little ball. He refused to speak and barely ate. His grades went from all "A" s & "B"s to nothing but "F"s. He refused to do his homework and often made me literally drag him to the car to go to school. He began to dress only in black always wearing a hoodie that covered his face and arms even if it was 85 degrees outside. He grew his hair out and refused to let me even get near him with a pair of scissors.

One day when he was off at school, I went in his room to gather his laundry and start a load before I went out the door to work. While I was in there, I began to straighten the covers on his bed, trying to create a little bit of order in his disheveled little life. I picked up his pillow to fluff it and found stuffing falling through stab holes in the back side of the pillow, inflicted by the open pocketknife I discovered on the mattress beneath. My heart grew cold. Fear flooded into me so fast I nearly passed out.

Ali Dixon

Later that evening I approached my son about my findings and asked him if he needed to talk. He just shrugged, refusing to answer any of my inquiries and resorted into the fetal position on the other end of the bed, head and face buried in his hoodie. I confiscated his pocketknife and left him alone without digging any deeper or even pulling up the sleeves of his hoodie to see what he might be hiding beneath; since, "obviously he didn't want me around and bothering him."

Days turned into weeks and I stood by watching my son whither. I walked into my son's room one Saturday morning to try to coax him out to share some pancakes with his family. Horror took hold of me when I found him draped unresponsive on the edge of his bed. I reached out for my son, afraid to feel the cold hardness of death I knew would be beneath my fingers. My heart in my throat, I folded his body in my arms. I felt warmth. He stirred. He was alive!

At that moment, for the first time in my life, God became absolutely *real* to me. I crumbled in a heap before Him and gave it all to Him. I begged for the life of my child and for the healing of his soul. I begged for the healing of *my* soul. In this moment I began to discover the *Secret Place* of the Most High.

> Perhaps it has been buried for ten years," she said in a whisper. "Perhaps it is the key to the garden! (The Secret Garden – Frances Hodgson Burnett)

> For in the time of trouble he shall hide me in his pavilion: in the secret of his tabernacle shall he hide me; he shall set me upon a rock. (Psalm 27:5)

It was later I began to realize that the *secret place* was not just a hiding place for times of trouble. The closer I draw to God, the more I give my life to Him, the more I realize the joy of the depth of that scripture …

> He that dwelleth in the secret place of the most High shall abide under the shadow of the Almighty. (Psalm 91:1)

This *secret place* isn't accessible only with admission tickets. I don't have to be suffering to walk through that door. God has invited me to live there, to make it my permanent place of residency. If I learn to really dwell there, I will have that intimacy with God that I've longed for my whole life.

> Then she slipped through it, and shut it behind her, and stood with her back against it, looking about her and breathing quite fast with excitement, and wonder, and delight.
>
> She was standing inside the secret garden …
>
> It isn't a quite dead garden," she cried out softly to herself. "Even if the roses are dead, there are other things alive. (The Secret Garden – Frances Hodgson Burnett)

That anticipation … that excitement … that wonder … That is what I wish to always feel while changing my soul's residence to *secret place of the Most High*.

42 - I Pray For You

How many times have I or someone else said, "I'll pray for you"? I have a prayer box where I keep cards of the names and prayer requests of those who have asked for prayer. The list gets longer each day to the point that my prayer box will soon be a prayer chest. The awesome part is flipping through those cards and finding the word, *Answered* written across the face of the card. It constantly reminds me of just how powerful our God truly is.

But even though we may be faithful in prayer, are we praying thoroughly? Are we praying also for ourselves?

> Praying always with all prayer and supplication in the Spirit, and watching thereunto with all perseverance and supplication for all saints; **And for me**, that utterance may be given unto me, that I may open my mouth boldly, to make known the mystery of the gospel, For which I am an ambassador in bonds: that therein I may speak boldly, as I ought to speak. (Ephesians 6:18-20)

Sometimes God overwhelms us with love for those around us. He piles us so high with compassion that we care for others and pray for others with no thought to anything else. But unless we take care of our own prayer needs as well, we may end up in more need of prayer than anyone else.

> ...Thou shalt love thy neighbour as thyself. (Matthew 22:39)

> For no man ever yet hated his own flesh; but nourisheth and cherisheth it, even as the Lord the church: (Ephesians 5:29)

Lord, I need You every day of my life. I need Your guidance in what I speak as in what I write. Lead me where You want me to go, and help me to be bold in teaching and praising Your name, Jesus. Help me to not only love and pray for others, but to remember to care for my own needs while I do it, both physical and especially spiritual. Without You I am nothing and I have nothing.

43 - Relationship

> If we say that we have fellowship with him, and walk in darkness, we lie, and do not the truth: (1 John 1:6)

Let's read that verse a couple of times and then let it really sink in. Do we have a true relationship with Christ? Are we truly in love with Him? Do we sit down and spend time with Him one on one?

The next big question is; does our life outside of our devotional time reflect that relationship? Are we a witness to the people around us? Do we make other people desire Christ?

Lord, please don't let me walk in darkness. I want my life to reveal Your light, Your truth Your love. I don't want people to look at me and be able to call me a hypocrite, because I teach the gospel and yet, live a lie.

Help me to demonstrate You by my speech, my attitude and my behavior daily. Let my speech be always with Grace season with salt. Help me to love my neighbor. Help me to be willing to give everything up for You.

I want people to see You when they look at me. I want to love You, I want to know You, I want to be more like You every day of my life. Let Your spirit dominate me from the inside out. Take my life and make it Yours. I love You Jesus. Amen

44 - Godly Sorrow

> For godly sorrow worketh repentance to salvation not to be repented of: but the sorrow of the world worketh death. (2 Corinthians 7:10)

Sometimes, when we as Christians lose our way, God, as a good Father must crack down on us and rebuke us. Sometimes He uses other Christians to give us the reminder, to jerk us back from the precipice we are overlooking and other times He confronts us directly through pricks of conscience, or other reminders. Either way, He makes us thoroughly aware of and sorry for what we have done. Just like constructive criticism when we are learning something or doing a job for someone, it is intended for our education, not our destruction. Like a father who spanks his child for breaking the rules, God must get our attention when we stray, or He wouldn't be doing His job as a father.

As a child we choose our response. We can either rebel, or chose to submit, repent and learn from the reprimand whether verbal or physical. When we choose to repent, God erases our mistakes right out of His book as if they never happened. Those sins are covered by the blood of Christ and cast as far as the east is from the west, never to be remembered by God.

Lord, when we mess us, help us to come to You with Godly sorrow. Help us to truly repent and give up whatever it is that we did wrong. Help us to cease and desist from that activity, and not run back to it thinking that Your grace will cover it over and over, so we can just keep doing it. Lord, I don't want to put false faith in hyper-grace. I want to earn Your grace even though You gave it freely. Thank You for forgiving me when I fail You. Let Your Spirit live so loudly in me that I know before I mess up and can more bravely turn away from temptations ahead. Help me to focus on Your Word so much that I do not need reproof because I follow Your Word no matter what.

Ali Dixon

45 - Springs of Water

When spring finally arrives and the snow begins to melt on the mountains, I drive each weekend up to check the Greenhorn Mountain road and the Bear Gulch road to see if the gates have yet opened. When the gates are finally opened, that is the sign that I can now climb the mountain heights and revel in the glories God has place only in the high places of His creation.

The roads are still treacherous in places as the snow has not totally disappeared and much of the road is rough and wet. In some places, ice still covers the rock making the way slick and dangerous. Streams of water from the melting snow flow across the road and down the mountain as they head to the rivers below.

As I maneuver over the rough roads, I hear this passage in my head.

> I will open rivers in high places, and fountains in the midst of the valleys: I will make the wilderness a pool of water, and the dry land springs of water. (Isaiah 41:18)

It is so exciting to be high on the mountain and watch God's hand in motion, fulfilling His promises to earth, to replenish. Even more exciting is to see the changes of season in our own lives. Over the past few years, I have literally, physically felt God moving in my life, opening rivers in high places and letting the water flow down, filling me up and relieving my parched and thirsty heart. He has taken away the dry, cracked hardness that was my heart and opened me up to love again.

Lord, always help me to absorb the love given to me rather than letting it roll off and on down the road. I don't want to be left dry and alone just as before. You caused springs pop up in my dessert. You have filled me with so much joy and a passion for You that it even tops the ecstasy that I feel when I climb to the top of Your creation. I praise You because You have done great things in me.

46 - Whiter Than Snow

Sometime the release of snow melt from the mountains isn't a beautiful stream as I described before. When we experience heavy snowpack and our spring is mild, summertime sunshine and heat causes sudden melts rather than the normal gradual springtime melt and flow. When this happens rush of melt can flow as a mighty stream, flooding where it will, guided only by valleys and the curves of the earth. The floods can devastate areas as the snow pushes trees and debris down the mountain into our river and streams, swelling them above their banks and into our homes.

> But let judgment run down as waters, and righteousness
> as a mighty stream. (Amos 5:24)

God describes judgement and righteousness, both as that mighty stream. Judgement washes clean, clearing the area of debris, wiping away anything that stands in the way of its cleansing. While Jesus' blood is the precious flow that makes us white as snow. His righteousness, first cleanses us of our sin and the debris in our lives and then covers us, seeping into our very pours, clinging to us so that God can see nothing but Jesus when He looks down upon us.

Righteousness doesn't happen without the cleansing.

> Purge me with hyssop, and I shall be clean: wash me, and
> I shall be whiter than snow. (Psalm 51:7)

Lord, because of You I am clean. The cleansing process is not easy, but it is worth it. Help me to continue forward not allowing any new debris to fill up my landscape. Help me to keep my life clean now that You have wiped away all the junk that filled it up. Thank You for cleansing me.

Ali Dixon

47 - By Grace Alone

Every way of a man is right in his own eyes: but the Lord pondereth the hearts. (Proverbs 21:2)

It truly saddens me when I come across people who believe with all their heart that they are good enough and have done enough kindnesses to get into heaven. The theory that a good person can work their way into heaven is completely contrary to the Bible. It is also sometimes the most difficult to witness to a person who truly believes that he is good enough.

The Bible teaches that salvation is not by works, but through faith in Christ Jesus alone. There is no selfless act good enough to earn us a place at the feet of Jesus. There is nothing on earth we can do that would top the sacrifice that He made when He gave up His life and His blood when He suffered and died on Calvary for us.

Understanding and acknowledging that Jesus is the one and only Son of God; that He came to earth as a baby born of a virgin, gave His life and shed His blood on the cross for us; died and rose again; accepting Him to live in our hearts as our personal Lord and Savior; is the *only* way we any of us can ever get to heaven, no matter how good we are.

For by grace are ye saved through faith; and that not of yourselves: it is the gift of God: Not of works, lest any man should boast. (Ephesians 2:8)

Lord, give us the words to speak when we encounter those who believe that they have no need of You. Help us to speak with tact and wisdom that only Your Spirit can give. Use us. Use me.

48 - Listen

When I was going through HR training, one of the phrases that came up constantly in class was, "Listen not to respond, but to understand." James 1:19 takes that training a step further in advising us to not only listen to understand, but also to be slow to anger.

> Wherefore, my beloved brethren, let every man be swift
> to hear, slow to speak, slow to wrath: (James 1:19)

When we allow God to be truly in control of us, we take the time to understand. We don't shoot from the hip and respond to situations out of anger, fear or spite. When we do not turn over full control to God, our mental reaction is slow, but our mouth goes full speed ahead.

As believers we should be sure to listen not, selectively, but thoroughly. When we hear only what we want to hear, we can create our own path and convince ourselves that it was God who gave us direction. When we do not listen thoroughly, we can fly off the handle and respond in a manner that does not pertain to a Christian, destroying work that God is doing or has already done.

Lord, slow me down. Help me to truly hear what people are saying. Help me to truly hear what You are saying. Help my responses to be guided by Your Holy Spirit inside of me. Don't allow me to be hurt or angered easily, but to take everything in before You decide as to how I should handle the situation. If anger is righteous and just, let me be slow to it, to make sure that it is You who have been offended and not just me or my pride. Lord, I'm listening.

Ali Dixon

49 - Consuming Fire

> ...let us have grace, whereby we may serve God
> acceptably with reverence and godly fear: For our God is
> a consuming fire. (Hebrews 12:28-29)

How can a God who claims to be Love incarnate, be a consuming fire that utterly destroys?

Deuteronomy 9:3, paints the picture of God as a consuming (or devouring) fire who would go before the Israelites into the Promised Land, destroying and subduing their enemies before them. We can look at the story as either a picture of God's wrath destroying everything in its path, or a picture of God's love protecting those who worship Him and follow Him, trusting that He will keep them safe and clear the path for them.

The confrontation between Elijah and the prophets of Baal on Mount Carmel is another example of God's consuming fire. The prophets of Baal called upon their god to rain fire from heaven but had no luck. After their crazy displays and pathetic pleadings to their god; Elijah built an altar of stones, dug a ditch around it, put his sacrifice on the top of wood. He then called for water to be poured over his sacrifice three times. Elijah called upon God, and God sent fire down from heaven, completely consuming the sacrifice, the wood, and the stones. The fire lapped up the water in the ditch. Then His anger turned against the false prophets, and they were all killed ... consumed ...

> ...Who among us shall dwell with the devouring fire?
> who among us shall dwell with everlasting burnings?
> (Isaiah 33:14)

Only the righteous can withstand the consuming fire of God's wrath against sin.

As it is written, There is none righteous, no, not one:
(Romans 3:10)

Then how do we withstand the consuming fire of God's wrath?!

Praise God that He has provided the righteousness we need by sending Jesus Christ to die on the cross for our sins. In that one, selfless act, Christ remedies the situation, satisfying the wrath of God, exchanging His perfect righteousness for our sin.

For he hath made him to be sin for us, who knew no sin;
that we might be made the righteousness of God in him.
(2 Corinthians 5:21)

All the wrath of God was poured out on Jesus, so that those who belong to Him would not have to suffer the horrible fate we deserve.

It is a fearful thing to fall into the hands of the living God.
(Hebrews 10:31)

Thank God, we don't have to fear the consuming fire of God's wrath if we are cloaked in the righteousness that Jesus provided for us by the shedding of His blood on Calvary.

Lord, thank You so much that You have spared me from the wrath of Your consuming fire. Thank You that You have covered me in Your blood, so God only sees Your righteousness when He looks at me.

I could never withstand the wrath of God for all that I have done wrong.

We have all sinned and come short of Your glory. But You have given us the greatest gift ever! I come before Your throne and kneel at Your feet, worshiping You with all that I am, with all that I will ever be, for what You have done for me. Thank You for the love and protection of Your consuming fire ... Thank You for sparing me.

Ali Dixon

50 – Provoke to Good

> And let us consider one another to provoke unto love and to good works: Not forsaking the assembling of ourselves together, as the manner of some is; but exhorting one another: and so much the more, as ye see the day approaching. (Hebrews 10:24-25)

When I first hear the word, provoke, I see one sibling poking at another, pulling hair, doing anything possible to annoy the other. I see people arguing about their political differences and causing themselves to believe that anyone who believes differently than they do are deplorable.

Webster also defines the word, provoke, this way, *to excite to action or feeling, to stir up, call forth, stimulate, to influence, incite to good.*

This definition brings several other scriptures to mind.

> Iron sharpeneth iron …. (Proverbs 27:17)

First, *it takes two to tango.* No piece of iron can sharpen itself. We must live life, not on our own, but in Christian community. When we become dull, it takes the influencing and encouragement of others, and sometimes the grating rebuke of a brother, to hone that blade back to a sharp and useful tool. We must have our brain stimulated by the thoughts and ideas of others of like faith. We *need* each other to stay sharp and ready for battle with the rulers of the darkness of this world. We need to encourage each other to live out and share the love of Jesus or we can fall into the pit of woe and self-pity. When we provoke another unto love and good works, we keep our own selves occupied with focusing on the love of Christ.

Another scripture that comes to mind is Proverbs 17:22.

A merry heart does good like a medicine." (Proverbs 17:22)

When we go around life with a smile on our face and allow the love of Jesus to shine out through our eyes, we lift the spirits of others. We become approachable, which leads us to the opportunity to encourage others, to lift them up. When other Christians see that our joy in the Lord is genuine and not just a front put on for church, we are able to encourage them to get in gear as well. We can be contagious in encouraging others to want what we have and ignite them to get moving in the right direction.

Lord, help us as a Christian family, as Your children, to provoke one another to love and good works. Help us to realize the importance of community, of taking the time to interact with those of like faith. Help us to hone one another and be truly contagious, encouraging each other to reach higher and go farther. Help us to lead each other by example and infect the entire Christian community. Help me to provoke in a good way, for You.

51 - Unperceivable

Oh, the majesty of standing on top of Lock Mountain, looking down over the valleys below! I close my eyes and hear the beating of wings as a hawk rises, the sounds of smaller, gentler birds chittering and chirping in the trees. I feel the fresh mountain air enter my lungs as I breath in the air around me. The scent of pine trees and nature permeate my nostrils. Standing there, absorbing the beauty of God's creation through all my senses is the reward earned for the long hike up the mountain to the peak. How could anything ever top this wonder?! How could anything ever come close to comparing with the mystery and the beauty found on the mountain top?

Isaiah 64:4 says that God is going to top His own creation, and I can't wait to see it!

> For since the beginning of the world men have not heard, nor perceived by the ear, neither hath the eye seen, O God, beside thee, what he hath prepared for him that waiteth for him. (Isaiah 64:4)

Lord, help me to wait patiently for You. Help me to serve others, waiting on them as though they are my master, bending and serving as You showed us by Your example here on earth. Help me to stand on that mountain top and revel in the excitement of You showing me more. Help me to remember to go to that mountain top when I get low and need to be reminded of what is in store for me when I leave this world and go home to You.

Lord, I'm waiting for You. I'm waiting to gaze upon the wonders You have prepared for me.

52 - What Manner of Love

I came across this scripture that has always made me wonder how Jesus, the perfect one, could sometimes be so seemingly heartless when He dealt with those who loved Him most.

Isn't He the one who said:

> What man is there of you, whom if his son ask bread, will give him a stone? Or if he as a fish, will he give him a serpent? If ye then, being evil, know how to give good gifts unto your children, how much more shall your Father which is in heaven give good things to them that ask him? (Matthew 7:9-11)

> Jesus said unto her, Woman, what have I to do with thee? Mine hour is not yet come. (John 2:4)

Over the years, each time I've read this passage I've always questioned in my mind thinking that Jesus was a wee bit harsh on Mary. I tried to place myself in her skin and wondered how she continued gracefully to tell the servants to do whatever Jesus told them to do.

How could she? She was human just like me. I can't imagine myself not breaking inside, tucking my tail and walking away stoically trying not to allow Him to see the tears welling up in my eyes. After words like that I would not be preparing for anything to be done. I'd be pouting.

But she didn't argue or demand or even walk away and leave well enough alone. She knew somehow that Jesus was about to answer her prayer in His own way and in His own time. She just prepared the way for the miracle she believed would happen. Why?!

It dawned on me! It was like I was watching the scene play out in my mind; like Ebenezer Scrooge watching the images of Christmas past, present and future playing out before him ...

Ali Dixon

Jesus was at a wedding with his disciples. His mother was there as well. This had to have been the wedding of someone special, probably even a member of their own family. During the wedding they ran out of wine.

Yes, it had to be family. Why else would Mary have known the situation and have been behind the scenes discussing the matter with the servants? She wasn't just a guest; she was tight knit on this one.

Jesus was kicking back enjoying this event with his disciples - his friends.

Mary walked up to Jesus and whispered the situation in his ear asking him for a favor, "Fix this please?! I want this wedding to be perfect, but we're short on wine!" Jesus, knowing she was the one person in the whole world who had absolutely no doubt about who He is and what He is capable of, felt warm inside because of the faith of this one precious woman.

A grin spread across his face and his eyes twinkled as he lovingly reached out and squeezed her, "Woman, what am I going to do with you?!"

Mary's heart welled up in her chest knowing when she saw that sparkle, that He was about to answer her prayer. It may have seemed like a small, insignificant matter to others, but Jesus knew how important it was to her personally.

She got giddy inside, waiting, not to see *if* the prayer was to be answered (she knew that would happen); but to watch *how* He would answer it.

The excitement welled up in her heart waiting for the *how*. She had faith he would handle the what but waiting for the how was the exciting part!

She practically danced into the room where the servants were preparing trays to carry out to the wedding guests. "Get ready, guys! He's about to do something big! Be ready and do whatever He tells you to do!"

Oh, to have that kind of relationship with Jesus … that kind of faith!

Jesus, I know deep down in my heart, that no matter how simple or insignificant my prayers may seem to someone else. You understand how important they are to me. Help me to prepare my heart for the HOW of Your answers no matter which way You choose to answer. I know that

You will answer me in the way that is best for me even if I can't see it at the time. Thank You for loving me and promising only good gifts in my life!

> Behold, what manner of love the Father hath bestowed upon us, that we should be called the sons of God. (1 John 3:1)

53 - Joyfully Confer

For many years I sought a relationship with God but could not find it. Repetitive sin held me back from having His blessing on my life. I was caught up in living in the flesh. He listened to my prayers, but I believe He heard them and sadly shook His head, mourning over the fact that I had strayed so far from Him that I deemed myself worthy of His grace when, rather, it was time for me to go roll in the pig slop and learn some lessons before I would repent and run back home to Him.

> But when it pleased God, who separated me from my mother's womb, and called me by his grace, To reveal his Son in me, that I might preach him among the heathen; immediately I conferred not with flesh and blood ... And they glorified God in me. (Galatians 1:15-16, 24)

> But as many as received him, to them gave he power to become the sons of God, even to them that believe on his name: Which were born, not of blood, nor of the will of the flesh, nor of the will of man, but of God. (John 1:12-13)

To confer is to grant or bestow something value such as a title, a benefit or a right. We see in John one that when we were born again, He conferred upon us the power, the right to be called the sons of God. When we are called of God, we must listen and obey immediately, returning that right to Christ, conferring not with flesh and blood, but giving over what we have spiritually to Jesus, doing His will and that passionately for the love He lavished upon us.

Lord, help me to walk in Your steps as a true Christian should do. You happily conferred the right upon me to become a child of the One True King. When I am called to do Your purpose, help me to return the favor and joyfully confer.

54 - Look Up

> My voice shalt thou hear in the morning, O Lord; in the morning will I direct my prayer unto thee, and will look up. (Psalm 5:3)

Spring Turkey season is quickly approaching! April 16th ... opening day ... I'll be Heading up to the mountains in the wee hours of the morning. I'll hike up the side of Lock and down into the narrow gulch where I've been watching the turkeys and tracking their signs.

Once I arrive at my special place, I'll remove the pack from my back, carefully leaning my shotgun up against the tree that will be my backrest for the next few hours. I walk quietly and cautiously out into the clearing and carefully place my decoys.

Bundled head to toe in camouflage so as to avoid the sharp eyes of my Turkey friends, I wait in the dark, patiently, for the sun to come up. Thirty minutes later I begin working my Turkey call waiting, hoping in anticipation for that answer.

I will sit for hours sometimes before anything stirs but when it starts happening all the hours spent under that tree in the cold just melt away as that Tom approaches and begins dancing for my decoy.

How much more divine when we wake early and place our sacrifice to our Savior, open His Word, and dedicate our time to waiting on a response from Him?!

We can't just sit and wait and expect an answer. We must make the sacrifice of our time and attention and call to Him and He will hear and respond in His time!

Ali Dixon

55 - Your Ways are Higher

> Therefore take no thought, saying, What shall we eat? or, What shall we drink? or, Wherewithal shall we be clothed? ... for your heavenly Father knoweth that ye have need of all these things. (Matthew 6:31-32)

Lord, sometimes it is so hard for us not to go into panic mode when we cannot see the finishing of Your plan. You know exactly what we need when we need it. Sometimes You put our plans on pause so that You can display Your more powerful plan for us.

It can be scary when we get down to the last dime. It can be scary when we have to pinch pennies until they scream, not knowing where the next meal is going to come from, not knowing how we are going to pay to put new shoes on our children's feet. All those things make the human heart quiver.

Help us to rely on You. Help us to have faith that You know what we have need of. You have promised to provide.

Hard times come to all of us. Help all of us learn to depend on You. Keep our eyes focused on doing Your will, knowing that Your will, will be done.

Help us not to want and desire the things that You do not want for us even when we have decided that they are the best plan for us. Help us to understand that Your ways are higher than our ways, and Your thoughts than our thoughts.

Help us to want Your will no matter what. Help us to not ask what we will eat or what we will drink or how we will be clothed. Help us to just trust in You.

Give us a heart that is so confident that Your plan will be perfect when revealed, that we go through each day joyfully anticipating what's coming next rather than worrying about what may not come.

Take our hearts and make them Yours.

56 - Tongues of Men and Angels

> Though I speak with the tongues of men and of angels, and have not charity, I am become as sounding brass, or a tinkling cymbal. And though I have the gift of prophecy, and understand all mysteries, and all knowledge; and though I have all faith, so that I could remove mountains, and have not charity, I am nothing. And though I bestow all my goods to feed the poor, and though I give my body to be burned, and have not charity, it profiteth me nothing. (1 Corinthians 13:1-3)

This morning's routine started the same as always. A fresh cup of coffee in my right hand, Bible, devotional and journal to my left, I sat down at the kitchen table and said, "Good morning, Jesus!"

I opened the devotional as I always do and began to read, and then began to cry. Oh, don't get me wrong. The author is one of my favorites. Her writing is always so motivational and up-lifting, full of promises of God's relentless love and other feel-good moments.

But this morning it lacked meat. Everything she wrote was absolute, Biblical truth. Yes, He will hold me through even my greatest disappointments. Yes, He promises forever pleasures in Heaven. His promises to His children are lavish and extravagant and so full of love, that they bring me to thankful tears ... often.

All I could think about is the fact that I was not put on earth for self-gratification. I am a foreigner to this world, a citizen of heaven, on a mission for God.

I believe that often Satan actually uses this new, watered-down religion that we live, to side-track us from our purpose. My life is supposed to be about doing the work of my Father, doing it with true love and compassion for those I was placed here to serve. Everything I do is supposed to be for His glory, not my own, and most definitely not solely for the reward. I have already been given the greatest reward ever possible. I have been washed clean by the blood of Jesus and clothed in His righteousness.

Lord, help me to love and live Your way. Help me to see our relationship as it ought to be, not a one-sided, pleasure seeking, living only for the reward, kind of love.

Help me to be the earthly embodiment of Your love for others, no matter how difficult it may be at times. Help me to live the strong life that can only be accomplished by diving deeper into Your Word and extracting the meat and not just sipping on warm milk.

I want to be vital to You, loving others and doing all You need me to do. I don't want to be a watered-down, sentimental, all-about-me, child, only in the game for the rewards.

Seek me. Find me. Use me.

57 - Walk in Wisdom. Speak with Grace

Walk in wisdom toward them that are without, redeeming the time. Let your speech be always with grace, seasoned with salt, that ye may know how ye ought to answer every man. (Colossians 4:5-6)

A while back, on a Friday evening, just minutes before closing, an elderly gentleman and his wife walked into the door bringing insurance paperwork from another company for us to review and quote new policies from. At five o'clock p.m., most of my coworkers bolted out the door ready to go home to their families for the weekend. I stayed behind and helped the customers, carrying on a lively conversation with them both while copying down their information and scanning all their documents into the system.

The following week, the gentleman came back into the office to issue the policies we quoted and sign documents. He was visiting with my boss while all the signature forms were generating. While he sat at the desk talking to Fred, I walked by the desk to pick up some paperwork from the printer. Our new client pointed me out to Fred. "That Ali is the nicest person. She was so sweet to us. My wife just really loved her."

Sometimes it is just as simple as that, being kind, putting on a smile and serving others with joy when all you want to do is go home and get started on your weekend. My behavior and willingness to serve this couple after hours, earned their business for our company.

Imagine if we lived that way always, conducting ourselves with wisdom, grace, and dignity to the world. Eventually people would have to notice the difference in us and hopefully turn towards God because of our true-life witness.

Lord, help me to always walk in wisdom. Let my speech be always with grace. Let my testimony and my willingness to serve, no matter what the circumstances, draw people to You.

58 - Cloaked in Him

> If we say that we have no sin, we deceive ourselves, and
> the truth is not in us. If we confess our sins, he is faithful
> and just to forgive us our sins, and to cleanse us from all
> unrighteousness. (1 John 1:8-9)

The more intimate we become in our walk with God, the more our eyes
are opened to our own faults. Things we shrugged off as, "that's just how
the world is today", come back to us as we acknowledge that sin is still sin
today as it was a one thousand years ago.

But consciousness of our sins is not intended to bog us down into
depression as we constantly flog ourselves, knowing that there is no way
we will ever measure up to deserve the love of our infallible God. It is
intended to initiate repentance. Repentance is the first step on our way
to living in His righteousness.

So thankful that my sins, which are many, are forgiven.

> ...but to whom little is forgiven, the same loveth little.
> (Luke 7:47)

Thank You, Lord, for forgiving me and allowing me to live cloaked
in Your righteousness.

Ali Dixon

59 - You Comfort Me

> And in that day thou shalt say, O Lord, I will praise thee: though thou wast angry with me, thine anger is turned away, and thou comfortedst me. (Isaiah 12:1)

I remember many times when I was young, doing things that were contrary to the rules of my parents. I was the child who liked to push the ticket but always got caught.

My dad believed that if you "spare the rod you spoil the child". But he also practiced the Biblical version of anger, "be angry and sin not". So, when I did get into trouble he never spanked while he was still seething. Sometimes I wished he just get it over with though.

I think the worst part of the punishment was not the spanking, but the waiting, with my hands on the bed, alone with my thoughts, while Daddy took his time in the other room, to cool down before coming back to administer my punishment.

I do not have damaging memories of those difficult moments with my father. For, although he was punishing me, I knew it was for my benefit, to teach me not to do that again, and not because he was a mean person, but because he loved me.

When it was all over, my Daddy would lovingly hold me in his arms and let me cry it out. Sometimes I do believe I felt a few of his own tears drop down on my head as he held me close in his arms.

Sometimes I need to just settle down and rest in the knowledge that God, like my earthly father, forgave me completely, and "although He was angry with me, His anger turned away so that He could comfort me".

Lord, thank You for pulling me up into Your lap and lovingly holding me in Your arms as my sorrowful tears of remorse spill out all over You.

Thank You for using my earthly father as an instrument of love in my life to help me understand the role that You now play as my heavenly father.

I'm tired of sin and discipline Lord. Today I just want to rest in Your strong arms, feel Your hand resting on my head and maybe catch a tear rolling down from Your cheek bathing me in the warmth of Your forever love.

60 - Afterward

> Thou shalt guide me with thy counsel, and afterward
> receive me to glory. (Psalms 73:24)

I've been noticing a lot lately in my morning readings that God has been pointing out the *aftereffects* of serving Him, almost as though He is preparing us for some big challenges ahead.

He never promises ease, a smooth path, or that we will be in a state of constant happiness. Sometimes joy may feel like a distant memory as we battle through our daily routines.

I find it comforting that God promises to be continually with us, constantly our companion, guide and support for the tough road ahead. He promises to uphold us with His strong, right hand.

Lord, help me to be prepared by constantly staying in communication with You, to be prepared for whatever lies ahead. Use me for Your purpose, no matter how difficult it may become. I know that when it is all over, and my work for You here is through, You will joyfully receive me into Your arms. Thank You for loving me every single day of my life. and giving me purpose.

61 - Balance

> Judge not, that ye be not judged. For with what judgment
> ye judge, ye shall be judged: and with what measure ye
> mete, it shall be measured to you again. (Matthew 7:1-2)

When I read this passage this morning, I envisioned a balance weight scale used to weigh out dry goods, gold, etc. It did not matter the consistency of the dry goods, the weights on the other side of the scale made sure that it was a balanced and fair measure.

Jesus cautions us about judging others. When we judge someone else, we are inviting God to judge us, to treat us with the same measure, meaning, we are inviting Him to use our same attitude and justice system to, in return, judge us for our actions.

The passage goes on to say,

> Ask, and it shall be given you; seek, and ye shall find;
> knock, and it shall be opened unto you: For every one
> that asketh receiveth; and he that seeketh findeth; and
> to him that knocketh it shall be opened. (Matthew 7:7-8)

Again, we see balance. Jesus offers us promises, *"ye shall find … it shall be opened unto You."* Those offerings are set on His side of the scale. If one truly pays attention to the rest of the passage we see that we have to put something on the other side of the scale to balance it out, to put in our own value to balance out what He offers, *"ask … seek …"* Every promise made by God in the Bible is conditional.

> But **they that wait upon the Lord** shall renew their
> strength; they shall mount up with wings as eagles; they
> shall run, and not be weary; and they shall walk, and not
> faint. (Isaiah 40:31)

Ali Dixon

The Lord shall fight for you, and **ye shall hold your peace**. (Exodus 14:14)

Honour thy father and thy mother: that thy days may be long upon the land which the Lord thy God giveth thee. (Genesis 20:12)

If any of you lack wisdom, let him **ask of God**, that giveth to all men liberally, and upbraideth not; and it shall be given him. (James 1:5)

Submit yourselves therefore to God. Resist the devil, and he will flee from you. (James 4:7)

If we **confess our sins**, he is faithful and just to forgive us our sins, and to cleanse us from all unrighteousness. (1 John 1:9)

If my people, which are called by my name, shall **humble themselves, and pray, and seek my face, and turn from their wicked ways**; then will I hear from heaven, and will forgive their sin, and will heal their land. (2 Chronicles 7:14)

As we go on and on through scripture, we notice that there is only one promise that Jesus makes to us that is unconditional, a free gift, in need of nothing on the other side of the scale. This gift is salvation through the precious blood of Jesus. For this promise He does not ask us to do anything or give anything, simply to open our arms and our hearts to accept the most precious, most expensive gift ever given.

How much weight do we want God to put into our requests? How much weight are we willing to put into our requests?

Lord, help me to live my life in balance, not asking for anything from You that I am not willing to sacrifice something for. Help me to always be willing to put in my fair share. Help me to remember not to be a taker wanting all from You without giving anything back.

I want to please You, and if I could find a way, I would add extra weight to my side of the scale for every gift You have given me to try to even slightly repay You for the precious gift of salvation that You offered to all of humanity. I love You so dearly, Jesus. I want to be like You.

62 - Desert Exposure

Thus saith the Lord God unto these bones; Behold, I will cause breath to enter into you, and ye shall live: And I will lay sinews upon you, and will bring up flesh upon you, and cover you with skin, and put breath in you, and ye shall live; and ye shall know that I am the Lord. (Ezekiel 37: 5-6)

Our bones are dried, and our hope is lost ... (Ezekiel 37:11)

My life has presented ample opportunity to ponder that potentially terrifying sense of desert exposure in both physical & spiritual senses that for me felt indistinguishable from one another.

A few years ago, I became dreadfully ill. It was then I began the journey through this terrible desert place of mine. It started with a trip to the hospital for what we thought was a heart attack, but ended up with Pleurisy, Pericarditis, and in the end, the chronic disease, Fibromyalgia.

My friends and family could not comprehend the pain I was going through. My illness was invisible to others, yet it began to dominate my life. It took months to heal from the first two illnesses, but then the pain never seemed to go away. I went through test after test but there were no solutions to my pain.

I spent the major portion of my time that first summer, contemplating ending my life that had lost meaning and no longer made any sense at all. I did not come home very much anymore. I would get off work and go straight to the mountains or my fishing hole where I would stay out all night alone in the dark with nothing but my thoughts, imaginations, fears and pain, praying for the darkness to swallow me up.

My thoughts ran wild. "How could God have let me down like this?" I had remained faithful to Him since I had come back home. I had devoted myself to the changes I had allowed Him to make in me. I had fully dedicated myself to my personal walk with Him. I was spending my mornings and evenings wrapped up in His Word and in worship.

But He refused to listen to my pleas for mercy and ignored the tears that fell from my eyes night and day. I fell farther and farther into a depression from which I could not draw my breath. The burning sun of this scorching desert was suffocating, dehydrating, dissolving me into a skeleton of dry bones.

During this journey through my desert, I experienced some of my most honest, introspective moments. I became very acquainted with myself. But I also became more acquainted with my Father. As I read through scripture trying to glean comfort and answers from its pages, I found desert stories, tales of other dry bones.

Hagar was a woman of extreme sorrow and utter desolation and brokenness of heart as she literally walked through the desert. When I found her story, I thought at first that it was a story of a strong woman of faith, an example of the strength I was supposed to have; a goal of who I should be in faith and dragging myself out of my desert. Hagar had no other choice but to trust God when her life and that of her son were on the line. A slave, taken from her native land, charged by her mistress to bear a child for her husband, and then cast out into the desert because of the jealousy of Sarah, Hagar was completely broken. Through her desert, Hagar found her fellowship with God, one-on-one, face-to-face.

> And she called the name of the Lord that spake unto her,
> Thou God seest me: for she said, Have I also here looked
> after him that seeth me? (Genesis 16:13)

Hagar met God personally, literally spoke to her Creator and yet she slipped away, back into her own life, away from God.

I think to me the realization of how Hagar in the future made sure to keep her son from marrying into God's family was a real slap in the face after she had been saved by Him in the desert. But then I got to thinking about it and realized why God used her as an example.

Her story was not about her faith at all, but about God's faithfulness to her. God, despite wrongdoings and botched plans, made a commitment

Ali Dixon

to Hagar. And it did not matter what she did with her life, He was faithful to His promise.

God has never failed me and will never fail me. It is I who turn away from Him, but He is faithful to forgive us our sins and to cleanse us from all unrighteousness. It doesn't matter what I do in my life; the seemingly dire circumstances that happen along the way. It doesn't matter how many times I have fallen away from God. He is always faithful to His promise. He will not take away the love He offered to me. He will not abandon me, leaving me forgotten, unseen, abused and rejected, thirsty in a dry desert. He made me a promise and He will always remain true to His word.

> Thus saith the Lord God unto these bones; Behold, I will cause breath to enter into you, and ye shall live: And I will lay sinews upon you, and will bring up flesh upon you, and cover you with skin, and put breath in you, and ye shall live; and ye shall know that I am the Lord. (Ezekiel 37: 5-6)

> A new heart also will I give you, and a new spirit will I put within you: and I will take away the stony heart out of your flesh, and I will give you an heart of flesh. (Ezekiel 36:26)

Lord, I have walked through my valley of dry bones, my own desert land. It is a place of painful reckoning, but also that place where I am found, uncovered and resurrected; brought back to life again by You. Thank You for taking away my heart of stone and for giving me a heart of flesh that can love and be loved, that can celebrate the desert places, rather than using them as a place of defeat. Thank You for healing my heart and promising me a new body, free of pain and sorrow when I get home to You in heaven!

63 - Rejoice – Pray – Give Thanks

> Rejoice evermore. Pray without ceasing. In every thing give thanks: for this is the will of God in Christ Jesus concerning you. (1 Thessalonians 5:16-18)

Three little commands that sound great on paper, can be extremely difficult to live, but make the Christian life worth living ... "Rejoice ... Pray ... Give thanks ..."

Rejoice!!!

When we rejoice, we make the conscious effort to put off our natural negative mentality and embrace the hope that is before us.

Many people confuse happiness with joy, when in all reality they are nothing alike. Joy is a state inside of us. It is something we hold on to and cling to even in the darkest situations. It is in fact, not situational. It is the piece that we hold inside of us knowing that no matter what we will be going home to our real home in heaven, to our Father, who will be waiting for us with open arms when we arrive. It is not a fleeting feeling brought on by pleasurable circumstances. So when we rejoice, we make that conscious effort to believe and wear that smile even when our world is turned upside down.

Pray without ceasing!!!

Jesus is our lifeline. When we pray continually, staying in constant communication with Him, it is impossible to ever feel alone or abandoned. Praying continually doesn't mean that we wear our knees raw from being prone on the floor, heads bowed, eyes closed, hands folded. It is a constant attitude of prayer, awareness of God's presence. It is whispering, "thank You," when things go well, and, "Lord, help me.," when things get difficult. It is the, "that was You!" when we recognize something only

He could do. It is the constant awareness of His presence beside us as we walk through our day.

Give Thanks!!!

Be thankful. This command requires us to step outside of our nature and surrender completely to worship God. It requires giving praise to the One who holds every moment of our life securely in His hands. Being thankful is not always easy. We must be thankful for past blessings but also praise Him for blessings to come, focusing on the hope that it's before us, even when it feels like all hope is gone. More than anything, it is trust, knowing that God *will* work everything according to His plan and for our good.

Lord, thank You for being You. Help me to live out Your will for me, Your purpose for my life, to rejoice, pray and give thanks., no matter the circumstances of my life. Without You I would be nothing. Therefore, I gave You everything … all of me for You.

64 - Depression

> ...Fear not: for I have redeemed thee, I have called thee
> by thy name; thou art mine. When thou passest through
> the waters, I will be with thee; and through the rivers,
> they shall not overflow thee: when thou walkest through
> the fire, thou shalt not be burned; neither shall the flame
> kindle upon thee. (Isaiah 43:1-2)

More than once in my life, I have suffered through severe bouts of depression. That sense of being lost and alone, the feeling that nothing matters all that much; the loss of motivation to put one foot in front of the other; can be so overwhelming. Depression is often looked down upon, especially by those of our own faith.

Depression can be viewed as a character flaw, a spiritual disorder, an emotional dysfunction and often blamed on sin in one's life. But there are many examples in the Bible of good, Godly people like David, Job, Elijah, Moses, Jonah and Jeremiah, who suffered through great bouts of depression.

David, the "Apple of God's Eye" went through so many highs and lows as seen through his story in the Old Testament and his poetry in Psalms. The drastic variances of emotion in that man may have looked like a form of insanity, maybe even as bi-polar depression. Like me, David made horrible errors in judgement. He sinned, he felt remorse, he got right with God, he slipped and fell again. But he always returned to the Healer.

> I waited patiently for the Lord; he inclined to me and
> heard my cry. He drew me up from the pit of destruction,
> out of the miry bog, and set my feet upon a rock, making
> my steps secure. He put a new song in my mouth, a song
> of praise to our God. (Psalm 40:1-3)

Ali Dixon

Job, on the opposite end of the spectrum, did nothing wrong. His depression came from testing by Satan that God allowed *because* he was righteous, and God had so much faith in him that He pretty much dared Satan to try to turn him away. But through everything, Job came out saying,

> Though he slay me, yet will I trust in him … (Job 13:15)

Jonah's depression was brought on by anger at God for His mercy to the "unworthy." Elijah experienced great spiritual victories over the prophets of Baal, and then ran off to the desert defeated praying,

> It is enough; now, O Lord, take away my life. (1 Kings 19:4)

Jeremiah went through constant rejections by the people he loved. He battled great loneliness, defeat and insecurity. He, like Job, stated the same thing to God in his plea,

> …I am in derision daily, every one mocketh me … (Jeremiah 20:7)

> I am as one mocked of his neighbor … (Job 12:4)

As with all of the Biblical character examples above, I learned through my own depression, that no matter what brought it on, no matter how dire the circumstances or how overwhelming the sense of drowning might seem, God is and always will be with me through it all. If I allow Him to work through it, the season of suffering that I go through, will not be wasted, but used by God in some way, to bring to good, to help others, to instill purpose and to make me stronger.

Lord, thank You for coming to me in my times of depression, not in a whirlwind, earthquake or fire, but in Your still, small voice, whispering gentle reminder to me that, "I am Yours and You are mine!"

65 - Where There's a Will, There's a Way

The old saying, "where there's a will, there's a way," I believe, came from the Bible.

> For it is God which worketh in you both to will and to do of his good pleasure. (Philippians 2:13)

When God lays something on our hearts to do, He also makes a way for it to happen. He gives us the power to perform the task He has assigned us to do, the work that truly pleases Him.

What is God's good pleasure?

> The Lord is … not willing that any should perish, but that all should come to repentance. (2 Peter 3:9)

God delights in our repentance, our obedience, our prayers and ultimately our relationship with Him. He loved us so much that He allowed Jesus, the reflection of His own radiance, His pride and joy, to be made sin for us so that we might be redeemed and returned to the image of Christ, the image we were designed to reflect; God's glory. He created us in His image, and therefore desires to see His own radiance reflected in us as He does in Jesus.

> Who being the brightness of his glory, and the express image of his person, and upholding all things by the word of his power, when he had by himself purged our sins, sat down on the right hand of the Majesty on high; (Hebrews 1:3)

When we become righteous, covered only by the blood of Jesus, when God looks upon us, He sees only the blood, the cloak that Jesus wrapped us in. If He sees His radiance reflected in Jesus, and when He looks upon us sees righteous, and only sees Jesus; His radiance reflects back from the redeemed, bringing Him even more pleasure. The more people we lead home to Him, the greater His radiance shines and the more pleasure we give to our Father who gave everything for us.

Jesus, we know that Your reflection in us, is what brings You pleasure. Help me to be obedient to You. Help me to grow and to pursue Your pleasures and not my own earthly ones. When I look into the mirror that is my life. I want to see, not myself, but Jesus looking back at me. Seeing You means that I am becoming more like You. Seeing You in my reflection means that I am reflecting the glory of God, reflecting His radiance, bringing You pleasure.

> But we all, with open face beholding as in a glass the glory of the Lord, are changed into the same image from glory to glory, even as by the Spirit of the Lord. (2 Corinthians 3:18)

66 - No

I am sure I'm not the only one who battles with that soul-crushing, guilty feeling when I finally must tell someone, "no."

People can seem so demanding. They know we can do or have the talent to do and so they ask. We know that God wants us to do our best in all we do, and our purpose is to serve. So, sometimes our own self-expectations are actually harsher and guilt-inducing than the actual expectations put on us by other people. We end up bogging ourselves down so much with promised performance for others; that we end up being crushed by the load and begin to grow resentful of those asking us to perform.

God does want us to help others, but not to the crushing of our souls. If we allow it to get so overwhelming that we become resentful, we are now no longer doing it in joy and happiness as God commands. Therefore, even if we do keep performing and serving, we are no longer in His will, doing it for His glory.

We must learn to say, "no," when the time is right. Of course, God wants us to serve other people. But we need to be reasonable with ourselves and with others. We need to reserve time to worship. If we get ourselves so bogged down with caring for everything else and do not take time for communication with our Father, we step away from Him and we lose focus on Him. Without that focus we cannot serve Him properly.

> Lift up your hands in the sanctuary and bless the Lord.
> (Psalms 134:2)

Lord, help me to be wise in the promises that I make to perform for other people. Help me to know when to focus on You, to stop and take time for worship and communication rather than performance. Remind me, with Your precious touch, that You are near, and that You bear the weight of what I am to carry, along with me. Your yoke is easy. Your burden is light.

Ali Dixon

Help me to remember that not all performance is performance for You. You do not assign me to bear the whole weight of the world. You only give me what I can handle.

I will take a break from performance, go into Your sanctuary, and I will raise my hands to You, and I will worship You. Guide me in the "yes" that I am supposed to choose and help me to have the strength to say, "no," when necessary.

67 - Heir

> For ye have not received the spirit of bondage again to
> fear; but ye have received the Spirit of adoption, whereby
> we cry, Abba, Father. (Roman's 8:15)

Many of the commentaries I have read on going from the spirit of slavery
to the spirit of adoption or sonship, seemed to be a story of entitlement,
what we will inherit, how great everything will be now that we are sons
of God.

But when I study on my own, I get a very different take on it. I'm not
saying that the inheritance, life in heaven when I die, won't be awesome.
In fact, when I was young, I made a cross-stitch wall hanging for my Dad
that said, "Working for the Lord doesn't pay much. But the retirement
plan is out of this world!" What I'm saying is that life may actually
become more difficult while we are living here on this Earth, rather than
miraculously changing for the better as many people believe it should,
the moment they become a Christian.

When we were born again, we were not only given the title of *heir*
but also a life of purpose a responsibility to the family. A servant or slave
performs their duties out of obligation to the master. They have no choice
in what tasks they will complete. They follow orders and check boxes off
a list. An heir, on the other hand, is going about the Father's business. The
job is not just a duty or requirement. It is done out of a sense of loyalty,
love and a true desire to promote the proud, family name.

I do not report to my work for Christ in a fearful state worried that
I will anger Him if I don't follow all the rules and do a perfect job all the
time. I go in with my whole heart knowing that God sees my desire to
serve Him and knows that my body was born human in that I *will* make
mistakes along the way. I move forward with a desire to please Him
and the comfort of knowing that as His child, if and when I do mess
something up, I can cry, "Abba, Father". He will step in to lift me up as
His beloved child and dust me off and show me the right way to go.

Ali Dixon

68 - The Perfect Work of Patience

> But let patience have her perfect work, that ye may be perfect and entire, wanting nothing. (James 1:4)

What exactly is the perfect work of patience?

Romans 5: 3-4 tells us to rejoice in our sufferings because suffering produces patience, patience produces experience and experience produces hope! So, in the long run, the final outcome, the perfect work of patience is *hope*!

Patience does not allow me to fight against my circumstances but to abide in Him, to continue in one place, to accept without objection, to bear patiently, to endure without yielding, content, knowing that God is always there with me and for me, working in my life and through my trials.

I learn to wait for His action in expectation, hope, calm, knowing that He will work everything out according to His plan and in His time.

Lord, as much as I balk at learning patience, I know that it is the only path to what I'm looking for ... *hope*. It is hard to rejoice in sufferings. But I'm trying to learn to greet each new trial as an educational moment, a piece of my journey, a character-building experience that will produce hope. Help me to abide in You, to take my strength from my connection to You as I wait for patience to have her perfect work.

69 - Like the Waves

I was thinking about the story of Peter walking on the water. He was told to keep his eyes on Jesus, stay focused, keep his faith in Christ without wavering; and as long as he did, he kept walking on the water. But the moment he looked down, he began to sink and would have drowned if Jesus had not reached out to him and lifted him up out of the sea.

Then I came across James 1:6

> But let him ask in faith, nothing wavering. For he that wavereth is like a wave of the sea driven with the wind and tossed. (James 1:6)

At first this brought my mind back to Peter and him wavering in faith. But then I got to thinking about the wave. James 1:6 states that, *"...he that wavereth is like a wave of the sea driven with the wind and tossed."* When Peter looked away from Jesus, he wasn't just drawn down by the waves, he became like the waves. He lost his footing. He had no foundation to stand on any longer. He was tossed about by the wind.

When we remove our focus from Jesus, we tend to try to blend in with the world around us. We become, *like a wave.* We lose our identity; forget that we are His own. We forget that we have His power in us to walk over those waves rather than to become a part of them.

Lord, please do not let us be tossed about and drowned by the circumstances around us. Help us to focus on the radiance of Your glory rather than being sidetracked by fireflies, chasing them into the dark only to watch them disappear and end up lost in the darkness. Help me to know that I can come to You in faith knowing that You will take care of all my needs. Help me to trust and not lose sight of You even when huge waves lap up between You and I, trying to distract me from my focus on You. Do not allow me to become like the waves that distract others and draw people down to drown with me. Use my focus on You to remind others that sinking or walking on water is up to us.

Ali Dixon

70 - Trust Me

The topic of my conversation with Jesus this morning was, *Trust me*. When Jesus speaks, His Words are so much more profound than mine. So, I will share with you the words He shared with me this morning.

> For I know the thoughts that I think toward you, saith the Lord, thoughts of peace, and not of evil, to give you an expected end. (Jeremiah 29:11)

> For my thoughts are not your thoughts, neither are your ways my ways, saith the Lord. For as the heavens are higher than the earth, so are my ways higher than your ways, and my thoughts than your thoughts. (Isaiah 55:8-9)

> Be still, and know that I am God: I will be exalted among the heathen, I will be exalted in the earth. (Psalms 46:10)

> What time I am afraid, I will trust in thee. (Psalms 56:3)

> He shall not be afraid of evil tidings: his heart is fixed, trusting in the Lord. (Psalms 112:7)

> Trust in the Lord with all thine heart; and lean not unto thine own understanding. In all thy ways acknowledge him, and he shall direct thy paths. (Proverbs 3:5-6)

Lord, thank You for Your words of comfort this morning. Thank You that I can trust in You no matter what. Thank You that You have a plan for my life and that even when I cannot see where the path is taking me, You are holding my hand and leading me. You won't let me fall. You are there to catch me when I trip.

When bad things come my way, You will be my peace. When good things come my way, You will be my joy!

Help me to walk through today completely aware of Your presence, completely in love with You, and trusting You with all my mind, my heart and my soul.

Share this peace that I found in You with everyone reading these passages of scripture this morning. I love You Jesus! I trust You Jesus!

Ali Dixon

71 - This is The Day

Looking out the kitchen window this morning, I caught a glimpse of the sunrise. Soft pinks, vivid oranges and bright blues shared the palate as God splashed them across his fresh clean canvas.

I reached for my camera so that I could try to capture just a small piece of His art to share with you. But along the way I noticed that the iced tea jug was empty, a bowl had been left in the microwave and there was still a sprinkle of flour on my kitchen counter that I had missed when I cleaned the kitchen the night before.

By the time I stepped out the door with my camera, the Sun had risen fully. The romantic, glowing hues of sunrise had melted away into regular, ordinary daylight. I had missed my chance to capture the moment. I felt a little saddened knowing the herd of deer, that I usually watch running through the alfalfa field outside my kitchen window, had already made their way through and already lined up and leaped over the fence into the neighbor's pasture. I missed it all over miniscule chores that habit just wouldn't let me pass by.

Disappointed I sat down with a sigh and opened my Bible.

> This is the day which the Lord hath made; we will rejoice and be glad in it. (Psalm 118:24)

Realization poured over me. I had missed nothing. I had seen with my own eyes the exact amount of splendor that God had planned for my day this morning.

Maybe that brief glimpse of His handiwork was to be my inspiration to enjoy each moment as He presents it. Maybe it was a nudge to make sure and pay closer attention a reminder to focus on Him rather than letting the routines of life get in the way of my relationship with Him. Maybe it is the anticipation I need to look forward to my next sunrise with Him.

Lord thank You for *this* day, *this* moment that I have the pleasure of spending with You. Thank You for Your beautiful reminders to take the time to rejoice and be glad in each new day and in each new moment that You give to me.

Ali Dixon

72 - Finish Line

> Wherefore seeing we also are compassed about with so
> great a cloud of witnesses, let us lay aside every weight,
> and the sin which doth so easily beset us, and let us run
> with patience the race that is set before us, Looking unto
> Jesus the author and finisher of our faith; who for the joy
> that was set before him endured the cross, despising the
> shame, and is set down at the right hand of the throne of
> God. (Hebrews 12:1-2)

Oh, what an example we have before us in Jesus! The author and finisher of our faith!

I've always read these passages focusing on running the race, setting aside the weight and sin, all the distractions in my life, avoiding the people and things that might get me into trouble and keep me from finishing.

But today, instead of the race, I read about the finish line, the joy that is waiting at the end of my race. Jesus is sitting there, at the right hand of the Father, cheering me on, saying, "Look what I endured for you! you can make it! Keep going! I'll be there at the end to hold you in my arms when it's all over!"

Lord, I'm running as fast as I can. It is so hard to be patient and stay focused. But knowing You are there, hearing Your voice along the way, sipping from Your life-giving water as You reach out and hand me cups as I run along the route, keeps me moving in the right direction. This race was not designed for the weak. I need Your strength and encouragement to endure. Thank You for being an example to me and showing me that finishing is possible. I'm ready. Help me stay the course.

73 - Purge Me

> Every branch in me that beareth not fruit he taketh away:
> and every branch that beareth fruit, he purgeth it, that it
> may bring forth more fruit. (John 15:2)

For some reason, I really enjoy reading about the vineyards and find it very interesting to know that many of the grapevines in vineyards go back hundreds of years and are still producing. The success of such vines is due to careful husbandry. After harvest, the lush vines that bore rich, green leaves and fruit, turn into ugly, dead looking sticks, good for nothing but firewood. But the unseen inside of those sticks it the valuable part that must be tended in order to enjoy a successful harvest next spring.

> But let it be the hidden man of the heart, in that which
> is not corruptible, even the ornament of a meek and
> quiet spirit, which is in the sight of God of great price.
> (1Peter 3:4)

Pruning is carefully removing excess material from a tree or shrub; trimming, especially to make more healthy or productive. Pruning is a carefully planned and executed process used to rejuvenate the vine, removing unfruitful branches and making room for new growth.

Purging is to clean thoroughly; to cleanse; to rid of impurities; to remove by cleansing, to wash away. Purging can be as simple as cleaning out our closet, our garage, or our desk … getting rid of things we no longer want, need or use … freeing up physical and mental space for the next season of life. Pruning is also a metaphor for courageously disciplining ourselves to get rid of habits of character that no longer serve us. Sometimes pruning happens when we must let go of difficult relationships. Each pruning and purging event comes with a certain amount of pain and some fear.

Pruning happens on the outside while purging happens on the inside.

Ali Dixon

It is very difficult to let go of anything that has been a beautiful addition to or useful in one's life. Often the things we are in most need of ridding ourselves of are things that we have invested our precious time and energy into. Memories are some of the most difficult things to purge. We worry that we may dishonor our past and are paralyzed by the *what ifs*. What if I get rid of this and then find I need it again? What ifs can cloud our minds until we are unable to prune away the dead things in our lives to the point that we allow the what ifs to suffocate and kill the connection of the branch to the vine.

When we purge spiritually, we clean out all the old junk from our spiritual veins and flood our roots with the living water, clean and pure, precious and life-giving.

> Having therefore these promises, dearly beloved, let us cleanse ourselves from all filthiness of the flesh and spirit, perfecting holiness in the fear of God. (2 Corinthians 7:1)

Lord, it's scary to just give in to You, knowing that You intend to rid me of all the junk in my life. It's hard to let go of things and memories that have been such a part of me for so long. But I trust You, as the husbandman, to be careful and gentle with me as You cut away all the trash and cleanse me, perfecting me for Your service. I surrender to You, Jesus.

74 - I Wait For You

> For they loved the praise of men more than the praise of
> God. (John 12:43)

How often do we find ourselves performing like puppets to a crowd? What are we doing? Why are we so focused on what other people think about us, on our outside image? Shouldn't it be the image that comes from inside of us that we are more worried about? Is that selfie so important? Do we really need the likes and responses from people about our outward appearance?

I would rather post a million pictures of Jesus love than even one of myself. I was not placed on this earth for praise of who I am. I am nothing. I am but dust, a broken piece of pottery needing to be repaired and made stronger, better and more beautiful by the grace of Jesus healing blood.

The only person that I matter to is Jesus. Everyone else can do without me. But Jesus loves me so much He doesn't want to do without me. He is the one that I was created to please. He is the one I will live my life for.

We as Christians should be focused on what God thinks of us, how He sees us. We should be looking for the approval of Him rather than the approval of mankind.

"As the bride waiting for her groom …" Jesus I wait for You!

Ali Dixon

75 - Your Plans Prevail

> There are many devices in a man's heart; nevertheless
> the counsel of the Lord, that shall stand. (Proverbs 19:21)

We devise all sorts of plots and plans, mapping out what we believe should happen in life, and are often disappointed when we find a rockslide blocking our passage. I have learned the hard way, that it doesn't matter what I plan or how I map out my life. God has a plan and a purpose for me, and He will see that I get to the planned destination even if I do detour all over the world on my way to where He wants me to be.

Saul of Tarsus planned to murder every Christian possible. But the counsel of the Lord stood, and Saul became Paul, founder of churches one of the most powerful preachers of his time and on into ours.

Lord, help us to understand that Your thoughts are higher than ours and that Your plans will prevail over ours every time. Help us to realize that You have already designed our life for Your purpose and that giving in to You is ultimately simpler than trying to do it our way.

Help me to listen to Your still, small voice as You guide me through life. Get rid of the stubbornness in me that wants me to make my own plan and design my own trip. Lead me, Lord.

76 - To Be Known By God

I am the good shepherd, and know my sheep, and am known of mine. (John 10:14)

Oh, how sweet it is, not only to know God, but to be known *by* God! He handpicked every one of us. He knows us better than we know ourselves.

My substance was not hid from thee, when I was made in secret, and curiously wrought in the lowest parts of the earth. Thine eyes did see my substance, yet being unperfect; and in thy book all my members were written, which in continuance were fashioned, when as yet there was none of them. (Psalm 139:15-16)

It amazes me that such a mighty God had His eye on me before I was even formed in my mother's womb. He designed not only me but what I would become. He penned my biography before I even came to be. He loves me and literally knows me from the inside out.

Oh, that I may come to know Him even a fraction of how well He knows me. That kind of love is rare and precious.

Thank You, Lord, for loving me more than anyone has ever loved another. Thank You for taking Your time, making the effort to truly know me. Thank You for promising Your protection. Just knowing that I will never be snatched from Your hand makes me feel safe, even when times are tough and scary.

I want to know You more. I want to love You as You love me.

77 - Dark Mirror

For now we see through a glass, darkly; but then face to face: now I know in part; but then shall I know even as also I am known. (1 Corinthians 13:12)

Years ago, I bought a huge mirror for my bedroom at the Family Dollar. Needless to say, it isn't the highest quality mirror in existence. It reveals enough to let us know if my makeup is complete or if Jack's hat is on straight, but it adds about ten pounds and twists and distorts the image just enough to make you doubt yourself and have to go double check in the bathroom mirror. We call it my *fun house mirror*.

Seeing through a glass darkly, brings that mirror to mind. Right now, here on Earth we have the Word of God and the Holy Spirit to bear witness of Christ. We can hear His words we can feel His presence in our lives. But we cannot yet see Him face-to-face. Our image of Him is distorted by our own human perspective. We cannot, from a distorted, partial image, fully understand and fully know our Father.

Once we arrive in heaven after our life here on Earth is done, we no longer will have to look in the fun-house mirror! We will see Jesus face-to-face and know Him fully as we are fully known by Him!

Lord You know my desire to know You as You know me. I wait in anticipation, hoping for the day when I no longer must squint to try in bring the full image of You into focus. I can hardly wait to see You face-to-face. But until that day I will not turn away from looking into the dark mirror. I will continue hoping to see Your reflection looking back when I gaze in. I want to know You I want to be a genuine reflection of You.

78 - Wisdom

> If any of you lack wisdom, let him ask of God, that giveth
> to all men liberally, and upbraideth not; and it shall be
> given him. (James 1:5)

My daughter and I had a very in-depth conversation the other day about wisdom. How difficult it is as a parent to adult children, to try and remind them of the wisdom that they have been taught.

God is so gracious to us. He gives us an abundance of wisdom if we simply ask for it. And this scripture says that He doesn't make us feel like idiots when we ask for it. Oh, how I wish I had the tact of our Father when I try to impart wisdom to my children. It seems that my conversations tend to result in tears and feelings of stupidity rather than wisdom.

Lord, I'm asking You for wisdom when I must communicate with my children. I do not want to make them feel inadequate. I want them to learn to be more like You. But it isn't my place to hand out wisdom. Wisdom comes from You and You only. Help me to share Your wisdom in a way that does not tear people down; in a way that doesn't make my adult children feel like I believe them to still have the intelligence of a five-year-old. Share Your wisdom with all of us in this family so that we may learn to communicate tactfully with each other, share our thoughts, and still walk away from the conversation unscathed by negative emotions towards one another.

> For the Lord giveth wisdom: out of his mouth cometh
> knowledge and understanding. He layeth up sound
> wisdom for the righteous: he is a buckler to them that
> walk uprightly. He keepeth the paths of judgment,
> and preserveth the way of his saints. Then shalt thou
> understand righteousness, and judgment, and equity; yea,
> every good path. When wisdom entereth into thine heart,
> and knowledge is pleasant unto thy soul; (Proverbs 2:6-10)

Ali Dixon

79 - Grace — Not a License to Sin

Righteousness keepeth him that is upright in the way:
but wickedness overthroweth the sinner. (Proverbs 13:6)

Years ago, I thought myself to be immune from sin's consequences. The idea that grace gave me the right to perpetually sin because God had already forgiven me was the worst idea I had ever come across, and probably had more devastating effects on my life than any other idea I had ever entertained.

The fact that we are forgiven by God's grace does not change the fact that sin has consequences. We are not licensed to sin because Jesus died for us and took our sins to hell. There is no statute of limitations on consequences. Lapse of time will not annihilate them. We cannot bury our sins, grow grass on the graves and expect that there will be no resurrection of what we did.

…be sure your sin will find you out. (Numbers 32:23)

Yes, when we are truly repentant and come to Christ for forgiveness, He is faithful and just to forgive us of our sins and to cleanse us from all unrighteousness. He does welcome us home and wrap us in his cloak of righteousness so that God can no longer see our sins, but only Jesus when He looks upon us. But the sins that we have already committed have put in motion temporal results that repentance cannot deliver us from. When we look at the life of David, we see the apple of God's eye, fully forgiven, pardoned by God Himself, yet living out his life suffering the consequences of his sins.

And David said unto Nathan, I have sinned against the Lord. And Nathan said unto David, The Lord also hath put away thy sin; thou shalt not die. Howbeit, because by this deed thou hast given great occasion to the enemies of the Lord to blaspheme, the child also that is born unto thee shall surely die. (2 Samuel 12:13-14)

When we use God's grace as a license to sin, we give way to Satan. We hand him the arrows to shoot at us and our Savior. We arm the devil for battle against our own Father. When we habitually sin, touting that God's grace is sufficient, we give the enemies of God reason to point fingers and turn prospects for Jesus away from the cross.

Lord, I know that I have sinned and that I have caused people to turn from You in the past. I know that I cannot escape the consequences. I cannot stop the snow-ball effect that I myself put in motion. I have asked for Your forgiveness and come to You on my knees in full repentance. I know that I have been redeemed and washed of my sins. I wear Your cloak of righteousness proudly. But I will never lose the sorrow I carry inside of me when I witness consequences in motion. I promise that because of my actions, because of the guilt I carry, I will work until my death to spread Your Word to as many as I can reach. I will do all in my power to reverse the damage I have done to Your name.

Thank You for Your forgiveness, Your acceptance and Your love.

80 - Mustard Seed

> If ye have faith as a grain of mustard seed, ye shall say unto this mountain, Remove hence to yonder place; and it shall remove; and nothing shall be impossible unto you. (Matthew 17:20)

> And the apostles said unto the Lord, Increase our faith. And the Lord said, If ye had faith as a grain of mustard seed, ye might say unto this sycamine tree, Be thou plucked up by the root, and be thou planted in the sea; and it should obey you. (Luke 17:5-6)

> The kingdom of heaven is like to a grain of mustard seed, which a man took, and sowed in his field: Which indeed is the least of all seeds: but when it is grown, it is the greatest among herbs, and becometh a tree, so that the birds of the air come and lodge in the branches thereof. (Matthew 13:31-32)

I noticed this morning that there are not just two passages that mention our famous little seed, but three. The third one speaks of the seed growing, not just remaining a tiny, super hard, little seed.

Something that impressed me about the verses about the mustard seed, found throughout Matthew and Mark, is the thought of power in numbers. I am a very visual person and therefore, I love to browse through photos when something sticks in my head. This morning, obviously, I was chasing that famous little mustard seed that we all know as a representation of faith. So of course, I went to the Google to browse through pictures of the mustard seed's end game.

At first, I found a few photos of giant mustard trees. But then, when I put it into context and searched the mustard plants of Palestine, I found that the mustard seeds that Jesus was using for a reference are in fact more of an herb that grows into a huge bush that grows sometimes up to fifteen feet high. But the tended fields easily grow as tall as a man before they are harvested. The splendor of the mustard fields is amazing. Tiny yellow flowers adorn the branches. Rows and rows of mustard bloom across the landscape providing shelter to the birds of the air as well as nectar for the bees.

Back to power in numbers ... if a farmer plants one, tiny, little mustard seed, what is the purpose? He will not have much of a harvest from one little plant. But when those tiny seeds are spread in numbers across the field, the farmer can make a good living from his harvest. As when believers join together in faith and in prayer, we can definitely move mountains that could not feasibly have been moved by one tiny person.

> For where two or three are gathered together in my name, there am I in the midst of them. (Matthew 18:20)

Growth is in the DNA of that tiny, hard, little seed as is our capacity to faith written in the genetic code of our DNA. God does not wish for us to remain a hard, little seed, dormant and useless, tiny and insignificant. He wants us to be rooted and grounded and to grow into a fruitful plant whose branches provide shelter for those seeking refuge, food for the thirsty soul and when planted side-by-side with others of like faith, use the power of numbers for prayer and good works, for love and compassion.

Lord, let our faith be more than just a tiny mustard seed. Help it to grow and multiply, producing fruits of Your Spirit. Lord our faith might start as a small thing but with Your guidance help it to grow and produce miracles. When You grow our seeds, Your works will be seen.

Ali Dixon

81 - Remember When

> Remember his marvelous works that he hath done, his
> wonders, and the judgments of his mouth; (1 Chronicles
> 16:12)

This morning I was thumbing through the prayer requests in my prayer box, praying again for requests not yet answered, and praising God for prayers that had already been. Tears welled up when I came across the request from a dear friend whose husband had been ill with cancer. Sadly, for those of us left behind, he passed away a few months ago. I cried for my friend who had been left alone to face this harsh world without her sweet husband. I asked God why He had chosen to take him rather than to heal him.

Then it dawned on me. God didn't shortchange him by taking him home. God chose to end his mission trip here on earth, heal him completely, and take him home where he would never again feel the pain and suffering from the cancer.

Looking back on prayers we have seen answered one way or the other helps us to hope for what's going to come next.

We aren't *just* supposed to remember all the marvelous, wonderful things God has done. We need to remember The times when we have fallen away from Him as well; times when His loving hand has not been so gentle; times when, as our Father, He has had to come down on us and correct us when we failed Him. If we let ourselves forget what it was like to be out of favor with God, we won't be aware of how much we need to stay the course.

Lord, help me to remember my experiences, both good and bad. Use them to keep me on track in my walk with You. Help them to keep me from veering off the path that You have laid out for me. Help me to remember prayers You have already answered and help me to look forward to the promises yet to be fulfilled. Help me to hope!

82 - Grace — The Fulfillment of Law

Over the years, I have noticed that the Old Testament is left out of many modern-day studies. Modern Christians tend to focus on the New Testament since the Old was written during the age of the Law and the new during the age of Grace. Modern Christians often believe that the Old Testament and the laws found therein do not pertain to them since we now live under Grace and are no longer bound by the law. But Jesus Himself asked us to pay attention to *all* of the scriptures, not just those that we find convenient to our lifestyle.

> All scripture is given by inspiration of God, and is profitable for doctrine, for reproof, for correction, for instruction in righteousness: That the man of God may be perfect, thoroughly furnished unto all good works. (2 Timothy 3:16-17)

In Matthew thirteen, Jesus admonishes us to pull out the old and the new as both are treasures and meant to be studied and admired.

> Therefore every scribe which is instructed unto the kingdom of heaven is like unto a man that is an householder, which bringeth forth out of his treasure things new and old. (Matthew 13:52)

> For whatsoever things were written aforetime were written for our learning, that we through patience and comfort of the scriptures might have hope. (Romans 15:4-5)

Some, more legalistic Christians go overboard stating that we must follow every law written in the book of Moses based on the scriptures below.

> For verily I say unto you, Till heaven and earth pass, one jot or one tittle shall in no wise pass from the law, till all be fulfilled. Whosoever therefore shall break one of these least commandments, and shall teach men so, he shall be called the least in the kingdom of heaven: but whosoever shall do and teach them, the same shall be called great in the kingdom of heaven. For I say unto you, That except your righteousness shall exceed the righteousness of the scribes and Pharisees, ye shall in no case enter into the kingdom of heaven. (Matthew 5:18-20)

If we were to follow the letter of the law as it was written in the day of Moses, we would still be offering burnt offerings to God rather than depending on the fact that that portion of the law was fulfilled and is therefore over and no longer part of the list of laws Jesus wants us to follow. Jesus fulfilled the prophesies of the Messiah coming to earth to shed His blood and die for us eliminating the works people in the Old Testament had to fulfill in order to make their way to heaven. Grace does not destroy the law but fulfils it.

> Think not that I am come to destroy the law, or the prophets: I am not come to destroy, but to fulfil. For verily I say unto you, Till heaven and earth pass, one jot or one tittle shall in no wise pass from the law, till all be fulfilled. (Matthew 5:17-18)

Lord, help us not to disobey Your laws just because You have gifted us with grace. Let us follow the instructions that You gave long before You joined us here on earth, as a sign of our love for You and as a form of worship. Help us to not pick and choose the laws we wish to follow, using grace for an excuse to sin against You. Help us to live out Your treasures both old and new so that we and others might find comfort and hope in them.

83 - According to the Pattern

Recently I was asked to create a crocheted item for a special order. A photo of the desired item was shared with me and I stated that I could, "come up with something similar," as I am accustomed to designing my own pieces and very rarely use someone else's designs. My customer graciously reminded me, "they do have a pattern for sale."

> …See, saith he, that thou make all things according to the pattern … (Hebrews 8:5)

How often do we as Christians try to re-create the wheel? God gives us a pattern. There is no guesswork involved. The instructions for our Christian life are clearly defined.

Lord, help me to let go of my desire to be in control. To make my own path and try to make it resembled what You have already designed for me. Help me to have faith, that, although the pieces may look weird and the pattern may feel *off* as I'm following the steps; You have tested the pattern. You know exactly how all the crazy pieces are supposed to fit together. Help me to have the patience to follow through to the end, when everything will fall into place and form a complete and perfect design that only You could've created. Help me to live my life according to Your pattern.

Ali Dixon

84 - Mourn Proactively

Coming from the human race and being adopted into God's family, we tend to carry with us baggage that we just could not bring ourselves to leave behind. One of those big things is our tendency to temptation and to place blame rather than taking responsibility for our own actions. The correct attitude towards our sin is found in James.

> Be afflicted, and mourn, and weep: let your laughter be turned to mourning, and your joy to heaviness. Humble yourselves in the sight of the Lord, and he shall lift you up. (James 4:9-10)

We as Christians tend to get it backwards, relying on human nature rather than the Holy Spirit to walk with us through temptation and opportunities to mess up. When we do end up in trouble, we moan and groan and try to blame the consequences that we face on other people or circumstances rather than taking responsibility and working through it in a Godly manner. We tend, not to mourn and weep for our sins, but for the condition that those sins put us in.

James advises us to humble ourselves and mourn *proactively*. When we come to the cross with a contrite nature and ask the Lord to guide us through temptations that lie ahead, He lifts us up off of our knees, and makes a way for us to escape rather than allowing us to flounder our way through.

> There hath no temptation taken you but such as is common to man: but God is faithful, who will not suffer you to be tempted above that ye are able; but will with the temptation also make a way to escape, that ye may be able to bear it. (1 Corinthians 10:13)

Everyone will mourn and weep. But it is our decision to do so proactively and live life walking with Jesus by our side, guiding us and comforting us through valleys of temptation; or reactively when we must face the consequences?

> Blessed are they that mourn: for they shall be comforted.
> (Matthew 5:4)

85 - Temptation

I have stomach issues that recently have made my normal eating habits impossible.

I grew up in Mexico and have a huge love for spicy flavorful foods … so this bland diet thing is killing me. (Or at least it feels like it). I go around with an empty hollow feeling in my stomach from not being able to intake the food that I normally do. I feel lacking and wanting most of the time. But I know that eating right is the only way to heal it.

Last Sunday, Jack made a huge pot of green chili while I was out taking a couple of hours break at the edge of my favorite fishing hole. Dual blessing!!! My man cooking for the family and a chance to go wet a hook after four months of not!

Anyway, as I walked in the door after my unfruitful but satisfying excursion, the aroma of his cooking wafted out the door and write up my nose. I know I'm not allowed to eat spicy. But a teeny tiny bowl?! That couldn't hurt could it? I know it's going to destroy my stomach but what do I do? You guessed it!

That one little bowl tore me to pieces, setting me back a couple of days, unable to eat anything again.

Temptation comes in many forms. Sin may look good, smell good, taste good … But eventually it will kill us. It will create holes in our lives, sores that will ooze and leak poisons into our soul that will eventually cause us to die from the inside out.

It is not the physical death, but the spiritual death that I am concerned about. I have lived as a Christian without Christ. It is the most hollow, empty, miserable feeling imaginable.

I never want to go back to that sickness again. I want to continue with the healing. I want to be whole again, able to eat the foods that are good for me that will satisfy me and fill me, I want to be able to eat the meat of the Word and not just sip on the milk of the Word as a I did when I first came back to my Father's house, filthy, ashamed, miserable and sick.

God has put His Spirit inside of us as Christians to give us that nudge of conscience, to let us know when something is not right for us, when something is sin. We know we should not take that bite. We know it's going to mess us up from the inside out. And yet, sometimes we give in to that pleasant aroma coming from Satan's kitchen as he cooks up a plan to destroy us.

Thank You, Jesus, that You are faithful and just to forgive us our sins and to cleanse us from all unrighteousness. Thank You that You, the Father, hold out Your arms to the prodigal and welcome him home. Thank You for washing the filth of the world off of us, for cleansing us and feeding us the precious meat of Your Word. Thank You for healing our souls and filling the void, the emptiness we had inside. Help us to resist temptation, understanding that no temptation comes from You.

Let the Spirit speak strongly and loudly to Your people warning us and guiding us and keeping us from sin.

> Let no man say when he is tempted, I am tempted of God: for God cannot be tempted with evil, neither tempteth he any man: But every man is tempted, when he is drawn away of his own lust, and enticed. Then when lust hath conceived, it bringeth forth sin: and sin, when it is finished, bringeth forth death. Do not err, my beloved brethren. Every good gift and every perfect gift is from above, and cometh down from the Father of lights, with whom is no variableness, neither shadow of turning. Of his own will begat he us with the word of truth, that we should be a kind of firstfruits of his creatures. (James 1:13-18)

Ali Dixon

86 - Vain Repetition

When Jonathan was little, he used to sit there while I was doing chores and carry on his own little conversation with me. It usually went something like this.

Jon – "Mom."

Me – "What?"

Jon – "Mom."

Me – "What?"

Jon – "Mom."

Me – "WHAT?!"

Jon – "I love you!"

I have a great deal of respect and love for my Dad. And my relationship with God is a father/daughter relationship, is it not? So, when I hear people praying, often I am turned off, not by the prayer itself, but the manner in which it is said.

When we come to Jesus in prayer, we are simply having a conversation with our Father. I ask myself, "How many times do I use the word, father, when I am talking to my Dad?" Does my conversation with him sound like this, "*Earthly Dad*, I went to work today. And, *Dad*, I had a really great day. *Earthly Dad*, I need your help. And *Dad* …."

> But when ye pray, use not vain repetitions, as the heathen do: for they think that they shall be heard for their much speaking. Be not ye therefore like unto them: for your Father knoweth what things ye have need of, before ye ask him. (Matthew 6:7-8)

Jesus, help me not to pray to be heard by people but by You and You alone. Help my conversations with You to be deep and meaningful and not clogged up with space-filling words that take away from our communication. I truly enjoy my conversations with You, and I think You should be able to take the same joy from them as I do. Help me to never pray out of vanity, but from sincerity, knowing that You already know everything, but are still taking the time to spend with me, listening to me out of love for our time spent together. I love You so much! Thank You for calling me Your child and giving me direct access to You.

Ali Dixon

87 - Great Expectations

> And not only so, but we glory in tribulations also: knowing that tribulation worketh patience; And patience, experience; and experience, hope: **And hope maketh not ashamed**; because the love of God is shed abroad in our hearts by the Holy Ghost which is given unto us. (Romans 5:3-5)

How often do we say, "I hope so," wishing something would happen, but knowing in our hearts that it never will? We've got it all wrong! To hope is to desire with expectancy and *believe that it is attainable.*

Ladies and gents, we must show our conviction when we use the word, *hope.*

If I, as a Dallas Cowboys fan, randomly make statements in my everyday life like, "I hope the Cowboys make the Superbowl," I am *making hope ashamed.* I truly don't believe it is going to happen, so making the statement that, *I hope* in things that I know or highly doubt will come to pass, takes value away value from the rest of my *hope* statements; "I hope in the Lord." "I hope in Christ's return."

> …I hope in thy word. (Psalm 119:114)

We may think that using the word, hope, incorrectly is just a silly, casual, everyday mistake. But we must, as messengers for God, choose our words wisely. People who do not believe that we believe in hope will not believe the message we bring of hope. It will be just as empty and meaningless to them as me saying that I hope I will someday win the lottery when I never buy a ticket.

> that speaketh truth sheweth forth righteousness: but a false witness deceit. (Proverbs 12:17)

> Let no corrupt communication proceed out of your mouth, but that which is good to the use of edifying, that it may minister grace unto the hearers. (Ephesians 4:29)

> For we are not as many, which corrupt the word of God: but as of sincerity, but as of God, in the sight of God speak we in Christ. (2 Corinthians 2:17)

When we hope in expectation of the coming promises, we are confident that they will happen and those around us begin to believe in our hope.

Lord, help me to be a messenger of hope in Christ Jesus, not in false hope. You have so many plans and dreams for each of us. Help us to stay strong in our hope and look forward to the end game with great expectation!

> For I know the thoughts that I think toward you, saith the Lord, thoughts of peace, and not of evil, to give you an expected end. (Jeremiah 29:11)

88 - Perfect Work

And the Lord God took the man, and put him into the
garden of Eden to dress it and to keep it. (Genesis 2:15)

Have you ever noticed, that even though the garden of Eden was created
in God's perfection, God created mankind and placed them in the garden
with instructions to "dress it and keep it"?

What needed dressing and keeping? Was it not perfect already?
Sin had not yet entered the world when Adam and Eve were given the
command to, "do the work".

Perfection does not create a state of idleness but always could stand
just a little tweaking.

When God sent Jesus to die on the cross and rise again, removing the
threat of forever death to those of us who accepted His perfect gift, the
perfect plan did not cease motion right then and there. Grace is a perfect
gift, full and complete. Yet God asks us to, *do*; not to just sit on our thumbs
and watch Him work.

One of my favorite Biblical mysteries revealed is found in a combination
of passages; James 1:4 and in Romans 5:3-5. In these passages we find that
patience's perfect work is hope. Hope is incomplete, still needing action.
Yet it is *perfect*.

God's perfect work does not happen over a day or a week or even a
year. He works in us throughout our lifetime expecting constant change,
growth and pruning.

Lord, help me seek Your perfection every day of my life. Help me
to understand that, although sometimes I don't feel like I am enough,
although I feel like I will never attain Your perfection, I already have,
because of You.

Your perfection happened for me when You died on the cross and shed
Your blood, took my sins to hell and left them buried in that fire pit so far
away from God's eyes that they will never, ever be seen again.

Thank You for Your perfection. Thank You for constantly tweaking me. Help me to remain moldable and not dry up and crack because I believe that I have, "attained perfection."

Help me to always remember that every moment of my life is a gift, a gift worthy of my laboring towards Your perfection.

89 - Cactus Flower

Trust in him at all times; ye people, pour out your heart
before him: God is a refuge for us. Selah. (Psalm 62:8)

Yesterday I walked out into the parking lot at work and was awed to see the elegant blooms of the cactus flower. Those delicate, gauzy petals nestled so comfortably among the harsh prickly spines and sharp spikes of the rough cactus leaves.

Looking at the flowers, I was strangely reminded of my relationship with God. He is a refuge for me. He cares for me so much that He provides protection from my enemies. Like the delicate flower among the harshness of the cactus thorns, I can thrive in Him take nourishment from Him, and feel protected knowing that no matter what trials come my way, it is God who is my sword and shield. Because of His great power, I need not fear what anyone can do to me. I am free to live and be who I am, a beloved daughter of the One True King. I can trust in Him for every need and He will not turn away when I pour out my heart to Him.

Jesus thank You for loving me, for protecting me, for giving me shelter in You. Thank You for opening Your arms and letting me pour out my heart to You. Thank You for holding me when I need love. Thank You defending me when I need Your strength. Thank You for being You. I am so proud to be Your child, a delicate flower, nestled in Your protective shelter.

90 - Your Love is My Reward

I grew up in a missionary household where money was always tight, but God always provided. Up until the last few years, I have had to pinch pennies until they scream. Keeping a roof over the heads of my children and food in their mouths has often been a challenge. But when people have reached out in need, God has always touched me to give what I was able, to help them out. And each time I have given, I have been blessed, even when what I have given has not been returned.

> But love ye your enemies, and do good, and lend, hoping for nothing again; and your reward shall be great, and ye shall be the children of the Highest: for he is kind unto the unthankful and to the evil. (Luke 6:35)

That's the whole point and purpose of our Christian lives. As Christians, we are to be like our Savior who *is kind unto the unthankful and to the evil*. We are told to love, no matter what.

Lord, help me to give, never expecting anything in return. Help me not to *lend* anything but to *give* with my whole heart. I know that You have a purpose for everything that goes out from my hands into the hands of another and for the words that leave my mouth into the ears and heart and soul or another. Whatever it is You ask of me, take it and use it for Your glory. Your love is my reward!

Ali Dixon

91 - The Shadow of His Wings

> How excellent is thy lovingkindness, O God! therefore
> the children of men put their trust under the shadow of
> thy wings. (Psalms 36:7)

This morning, as it was spending time in the Word, I was strongly impressed by the image this passage brought into my imagination. Always before this passage of scripture has given me the picture of a tiny little bird huddled afraid and cold under the comforting wing of his mother as they huddled together on a branch. But this morning I had a completely different picture of putting my trust under the shadow of His wing.

I pictured an eagle soaring high over the caverns drifting in the air currents watching with keen eyes, all the activities below. I imagined the wind in his face as he soared through the sky swooping down low over a river and then beating his powerful wings to climb back up into the air, raising higher and higher. I could feel the exhilaration of flight, of freedom, of power!

When we put our trust under the shadow of His wings, it is impossible to just sit still and stagnate. We can't brood over difficult circumstances or wallow in self-pity.

The shadow of His wings is constantly in motion. We soar with Him. We climb to new heights that we never dreamed imaginable. Under the shadow of His wings, our strength is renewed. We are no longer weak and insignificant.

Lord, thank You for the image You placed on my heart today. Thank You for showing me that being under the shadow of Your wings is not like being under someone's thumb. It is a freedom that is unimaginable until one experiences it. Thank You for causing me to fly! Thank You for letting me see the world and humanity from Your perspective. Help me to always remember to stay in motion with You rather than huddling scared and afraid in someone else's shadow. I love You so much, Jesus! Amen.

92 - I Give it All to You

Last night after a long day at work, then coming home, cooking dinner, and cleaning the kitchen, I walked outside to fit just two more chores into my insane schedule before darkness allowed no more.

I went to the garden, started the watering, then stepped into the swimming pool, scrub brush in hand, to remove some of the green algae that the recent rains had triggered. I scrubbed until my shoulders hurt, then laid down the brush up along the side of the pool, kicked back and laid on the surface of the water, allowing all my weary muscles to simply relax.

As I lay there drifting slowly across the surface of the water, I talk to God about all of the frustrations, all of the disappointments, all of the desires that are so built up inside of me; that sometimes I feel I'm going to burst from the pressure of it all taking up so much space inside of my heart.

I laid there for quite a while watching the clouds float by moving into different formations as the moon seemed to float, yet remain fixed, faithfully, right there in the center of the moving artwork that God was forming before my eyes. Isaiah 55:8 & 9 repeated itself in my mind and in my heart.

> For my thoughts are not your thoughts, neither are your ways my ways, saith the Lord. For as the heavens are higher than the earth, so are my ways higher than your ways, and my thoughts than your thoughts. (Isaiah 55:8-9)

Lord I give it all to You. I know You have a special plan for my life, and although it may seem random and haphazard to anyone looking from the outside in, I know that, like those drifting clouds formed into beautiful paintings, so my life will be something beautiful, that will bless the right person, who takes a moment to look, in Your perfect time. And like that moon, You will remain steady and faithful, centered in the constant motion and commotion that is my life. Help me to let go and rest in the fact that You have it all planned out.

Ali Dixon

93 - I Can If You Can

I was reading the story of the boy with the demon, in Mark chapter nine this morning. I have always read the part, *Lord, I believe ... help my unbelief,* and have repeated that phrase a million times over in my life.

But what stood out to me this morning was the challenge from the boy's father, *if You can,* and then Jesus' response.

I can just see the look on Jesus face. He walked in, the most powerful creature in the universe, God, recognized immediately by the demon inside of the boy, and yet challenged by a mere mortal man ... **If You can** .... I don't think the boy's father meant to insult Jesus. But I do believe that Jesus felt a pain inside His heart, that His own creation did not even acknowledge His power or who He is. I know a thousand times, at least, that I have been told I cannot do something. My immediate response is always, "watch me!" followed up by, "Pretty good for a girl! Huh?!"

It had to be hard for Jesus, the one and only Son of God, to leave His throne of glory, where angels bowed at His feet and did His bidding, come here to Earth where He was unrecognized and even hated and then to have one of His own people challenge His abilities as God ... *if You can.*

I love Jesus response ... "*if **you** can ....*"

As much as I am sure Jesus wanted to reveal His majesty, knowing He could simply snap His fingers and make the whole world right, Jesus turned the challenge back to mankind, "*I can if you can ... believe ... simply believe*".

Lord You don't ask much of us after You gave all of Yourself for us. The simplicity of Your challenge to mankind sometimes seems so complex. *believe.* I know You can do any and all things. Help me to increase my faith so that when challenged to prove You, I have the ability to respond ... "*I can ... because I believe.*"

94 - Corporate Prayer

I've been thinking a lot about the power of prayer and the power of us, as a church body, gathering together to pray. I began reading from Matthew 18:20, touting my knowledge of the passage to myself, believing myself to be armed for battle on the subject of corporate prayer.

> For where two or three are gathered together in my name, there am I in the midst of them. (Matthew 18:20)

But, I, as many others, have been reading that passage out of context for many years. When I was reading through the entire chapter this morning, it dawned on me that the context of this passage addresses church discipline of a sinning member, not corporate prayer.

Often Christians believe that this passage give them the ability to be able to ask God for anything with the expectation that He will answer according to the desired outcome; often in the end, causing Christians to throw their fists in God's face when prayers are not magically answered according to their wishes.

Yes, Jesus is present and very pleased when people pray together. But He is equally present when we come to Him privately.

> Not forsaking the assembling of ourselves together, as the manner of some is; but exhorting one another: and so much the more, as ye see the day approaching. (Hebrews 10:25)

> But thou, when thou prayest, enter into thy closet, and when thou hast shut thy door, pray to thy Father which is in secret; and thy Father which seeth in secret shall reward thee openly. (Matthew 6:6)

Corporate prayer is not about the gathering of numbers, but

cooperating with God, setting aside the weight and sins that so easily beset us. Corporate prayer, joins the body, binding us closer together for God's purpose. It opens our hearts to the needs of others bringing accountability, edification, joy, encouragement and repentance.

> And if one prevail against him, two shall withstand him; and a threefold cord is not quickly broken. (Ecclesiastes 4:12)

Over the years I have learned to never want anything more than God wants it. And although we gather in corporate prayer over a particular need, sometimes God's answers do not seem to make sense. He has a perfect plan that even corporate prayer is not going to change. His plan will one day be revealed and the end of it, whatever that may be, will be for His glory.

Lord, I need the fellowship of the brethren to lift me and encourage me to be a better, stronger, more powerful part of the Body of Christ. I need to be joined together with other believers, always in likeminded prayer for Your will, not ours, to be done. I love my private, one-on-one conversations with You. But the community of believers who surround me have become my stability, my encouragement to stay the course. Thank You for providing for me a cord that is not easily broken. Thank You for placing me in the path of other believers who are willing to align with me and with You in corporate prayer for each other, knowing that Your thoughts are higher than ours and that Your plan will be fulfilled in Your way, in Your time and for Your glory. Thank You for not making me do life alone.

95 - My Times Are In Your Hands

This morning while reading my daily devotions I could not find my focus. So, I began to prayerfully flip through the pages of my Bible, letting my eye fall where it would, on verses I have highlighted or underlined throughout my studies.

Psalm thirty-one fell open and I began to read until verse fifteen popped out at me, *"My times are in thy hand ..."*

I continued to browse through scripture, then picked up a devotional book I like to read every day to give me a kick start. I had already read the devotion for today, so, I flipped back to Sunday's devotion since I had skipped it in my hurry to get out the door to church. There again ... Psalm 31:15, *"My times are in thy hand."*

God obviously wants me to think on that passage for some reason. As I prayed over that scripture, my mind went back to kind of a side topic that pastor Charlie included in his sermon a while back. During the course of his sermon about the faithfulness of Joseph, he described Joseph's father, Jacob. He described how he lived with death on his mind.

He was the beloved son of Isaac. Yet he was afraid to live. When Joseph was taken from him, Jacob thought he would die. When Joseph (now second in command in Egypt), requested Benjamin be brought before him, again Jacob thought it would be the death of him.

When Joseph presented Jacob to Pharaoh, even then, Jacob complained that he had not reached the length of life that his fathers before him had and yet he was still alive.

God does not want us to live with death in mind. He has a purpose for us here on Earth and whether our days here on Earth are many or few, we are to use them focused on fulfilling the mission that Jesus gave us, rather than planning for the end of our lives or even the afterlife.

Ali Dixon

I believe that many Christians today are so focused on getting to heaven with all its blessings and rewards, that we forget why we are here. The purpose of our lives here on earth is not to attain rewards. The rewards that we are promised are for the end game only.

We need to be focused on the journey, the now, what we can do here on Earth to repay Jesus as much as is possible for the precious gift He has *already* given us, Salvation.

I have had many Christians tell me that I am wrong for asking the Lord not to come back just yet. They don't seem to understand my feelings on this subject. Yes, I desperately want to go home to heaven, to walk and talk with Jesus, to experience no more pain or sorrow ever. But I cannot imagine being there without all the people that I love. There are so many who would be left behind because they have not yet asked Jesus into their hearts.

The pain of leaving them behind, for me, far outweighs the thought of the joy of going to heaven now and leaving behind the hardships I face here. I find the best description of my feelings on this subject in Philippians.

> For I am in a strait betwixt two, having a desire to depart, and to be with Christ; which is far better: Nevertheless to abide in the flesh is more needful for you. Lord. (Philippians 1:23-24)

I ask that You help me to use my time here wisely for You. My times are most definitely in Your hands. I pray that You will give me the heart of Jesus to realize that the more time I spend here, the more opportunity You give me to spread Your Word, to saturate the hearts of others with Your love, to lead others home to You.

> The Lord is not slack concerning his promise, as some men count slackness; but is longsuffering to us-ward, not willing that any should perish, but that all should come to repentance. (2 Peter 3:9)

Help me to not live as Jacob with death on my mind, but to rest comfortably, knowing that You have my life completely planned out; knowing that *"my times are in Your hands"*.

Cloaked

96 - Let Me Be Your Fire

> Hear me, O Lord, hear me, that this people may know
> that thou art the Lord God, and that thou hast turned
> their heart back again. (1 Kings 18:37)

Elijah had dared the prophets of Baal to prove whose god was greater. The prophets of Baal could not for the life of them call down fire from heaven to burn their sacrifice. Elijah taunted them for hours asking them if their god was on vacation or asleep.

In order to make the power of our God more evident than it already was; Elijah pushed the ticket on his preparation for God to bring down fire from heaven. Twelve barrels of water had been poured over the sacrifice, the wood, the alter. The trench around the alter was full and overflowing. Everything was saturated and had soaked in thoroughly.

> Then the fire of the Lord fell, and consumed the burnt
> sacrifice, and the wood, and the stones, and the dust, and
> licked up the water that was in the trench. (1 Kings 18:38)

How amazingly exciting! Every time I read the story; I feel a thrill run through my whole body. How I wish I could have been a fly on the wall to watch this whole event transpire. Oh, how I would love to witness the power of God in such an obvious, visual statement.

We are in a very similar situation today as Elijah was in way back then. We are in a drought, not a physical drought but a spiritual drought. We have not rejected God in words as the prophets of Baal had, but we have weeded Him out of our lives. He is our church day God and that is all. We may worship Him, but He is not the only one we worship. We idolize people, popularity, success, etc. We put Him on the same level as a million other little things in our lives. He is a trophy to be display and praised when the right opportunity presents itself but left on the mantle to gather dust until we have time or occasion to pay attention to Him again.

Lord, we need a miracle. Help us to see You for who You are. Help us to put You in perspective and lift You high on the pedestal where You belong. Help us to realize that we cannot serve two masters. Maybe You are not so blatantly obvious in Your participation in our day and age. Maybe we cannot call down fire from heaven to consume our saturated offerings to You. But we call on You to wake up this generation. Answer us and show us how You want us to move and what You want us to do. Help our lives be the demonstration of Your power that others need to see. Help us to be Your all-consuming fire here on earth.

97 - Salt

> Ye are the salt of the earth: but if the salt have lost his
> savour, wherewith shall it be salted? it is thenceforth good
> for nothing, but to be cast out, and to be trodden under
> foot of men. (Matthew 5:13)

What characteristics do salt and Christians have in common? Why would Jesus use a chemical compound to parallel the Christian life? And why would He talk about salt losing its savor when it is so stable and cannot, by nature, be changed?

I believe Jesus used salt as an example because of its very distinctive characteristics.

First of all, salt cannot be changed but can be diluted, as a Christian, once born again, cannot be unborn. We can never lose our salvation no matter what we do or how hard we may turn our backs on God.

Jesus warns us as Christians to not lose the characteristics and qualities that bring light and life to this dark and dying world; the characteristics of Jesus that flavor the world. If we set aside our values, our morals, the teachings of Scripture, we become worthless as Christians. We no longer serve the purpose God intended us for. We are useless to perform the mission that God gave us.

When trodden under foot, a single grain of salt mixes in with the dirt and cannot be distinguished from the grains of dirt around it. We as Christians can allow ourselves to be trodden down, ashamed of the Gospel of Christ, and become indistinguishable from the world around us.

> And be not conformed to this world: but be ye
> transformed … (Romans 12:2)

Salt has been used for ages, to preserve food. Salt dries food, drawing water out of it, dehydrating it causing it to last much longer without the chance of it turning into a science experiment. As we know, all living things require water to survive. Nothing, including, bacteria, can grow without it.

We as Christians are also preservers of good, moral disinfectants per se. We are to lead by example, love those around us (especially the most unlovable). Our treatment of and demeanor with others is a model to the world of how our Father is. If we do not behave well, we are a terrible example to others of who Jesus truly is. We must maintain clean morals and a clean mouth. When we live Jesus' purpose and by His example, we draw the life out of any accusations that are placed against us that would shame our heavenly Father.

> For the name of God is blasphemed among the Gentiles through you ... (Romans 2:24)

Salt can enhance and bring out other flavors. It adds just the right kick to a dish making a good flavor great. We as Christians are to be agents of change. We need to be edifying, lifting others, encouraging them to use their God-given talent, encouraging their flavors to really pop. We must spice up this bland world with the Gospel of Jesus.

Do you remember that old Kramer line, "These pretzels are making me thirsty"? Salt in the mouth dries it out making us thirsty. We as Christians should be the salt in the mouths of the world around us. We should, by the way we live, make others thirst for what we have that makes us different, making them thirst for the Living Water.

One grain of salt alone cannot create near the change that many grains, gathered together can. When we stand together as a community, the changes that are possible are countless.

Lord, help us to be salty for You. Help us to be a flavor that stands out and makes the world thirsty for You. Help us not to be washed out and blend into society so that we are indistinguishable from those around us. Help us not to lose our savor.

98 - Too Salty

Jack loves bacon! A while back he started ordering entire slabs from an online retailer and having me slice the slabs on our meat slicer into thick cuts, probably about three times as thick as the store-bought slices. I must admit, it was delicious, and did not curl upon frying. He was hooked. But then something happened. The last batch he ordered (and I do mean last) was so salty he could not stand to eat it as he had done the previous order. It was only good to be diluted in a pot of beans or cooked in small amounts and mixed in with other ingredients. It turned from a delicious breakfast bounty, to an additive, a seasoning that could only be eaten in very small portions and well diluted.

Sometimes our zealousness for Christ can come off as overpoweringly salty. We can ruin the beautiful thing that God intended in our eagerness to be distinct and separate. We often too easily judge others, wielding Scripture as a weapon, allowing our fear of things we do not approve of dictate our often unkind, prejudicial and hurtful reactions to people.

We mask the fragrant ingredients of God's grace, mercy and justice with the intensity and strength of our salty reactions. When our message becomes overbearingly salty, we become unpalatable. And God's message does not come off as He intended.

We are warned in Scripture that although we are to be the salt of the earth, we should never allow ourselves to become too salty.

> But sanctify the Lord God in your hearts: and be ready always to give an answer to every man that asketh you a reason of the hope that is in you **with meekness and fear**: (1 Peter 3:15)

> Him that is weak in the faith receive ye, but not to doubtful disputations ... But why dost thou judge thy brother? or why dost thou set at nought thy brother? for we shall all

Ali Dixon

stand before the judgment seat of Christ ... For meat destroy not the work of God ... (Romans 14:1,10, 20)

Lord, help me witness not to be so overpowering that it turns people away from You. Help me to be just salty enough to make people thirst for more of You, but not so much that I dry up their desire to seek You out.

99 - God Is With Us

...Fear ye not, stand still, and see the salvation of the
Lord ... (Exodus 14:13)

This morning my mind is playing the fly-on-the-wall game it loves to play,
watching as a scene plays out in the Bible as though I am there actually
seeing it happen.

As I hovered there watching the children of Israel standing, the
mighty sea in front of them and the Egyptians closing in on their rear.
I can see the panic on each face, fear that this is the end. They begin to
lash out at Moses, angry that he dragged them out from slavery to death.
But then God opened up the sea and allowed them to walk into it on dry
ground.

Faces changed from fear and anger to fear and awe. Can you imagine
the fright of walking between those walls of water, knowing God has
said that He will save you from drowning, but with human heart fearing
that those walls of water will fall in on you and drown you? They had
to have been in fear that their cursing of Moses and cursing of God for
taking them out into the wilderness was about to be repaid while in the
middle of the sea. I know I would have been shaking in my boots for fear
of righteous punishment from an angry God.

But God kept His promise. As the Israelites pushed forward, the cloud
stayed between them and the Egyptians so that neither side could see each
other. It served as frustration to the Egyptians, and peace to the Israelites
as they faced the fear ahead of them and on the sides of them. God blocked
them from seeing what was behind because He knew that as humans, that
extra, added fear would be the death of them. But the Egyptians brazenly
followed the Israelites into the sea, still divided by that wall of cloud, but
pushing forward as the Israelites progressed on to the other side.

I really love the next scene. God peeks through the curtain at the
Egyptians to see how they are doing about coming through the sea and
then begins to torment them; causing wheels to fall from their chariots

Ali Dixon

giving them all kinds of issues. I can imagine instant mud appearing and sucking their feet in making it nearly impossible to take a step. I can see their deadly rage turning to total confusion and terror as the terrain beneath their feet suddenly begins to change and water walls begin to spring leaks. I don't believe it was a quick sweeping death, because God said, *"The Egyptians shall know ..."* It must have been like one of those terrible nightmares I sometimes experience, where I know I am in danger, but nothing I can do will help me to escape. My movements are in slow motion, but the enemy is moving fast towards me. The Egyptians, in this moment were well aware that God was fighting for Israel and became petrified, knowing they had messed up, and this time fatally.

> ...the Egyptians said, Let us flee from the face of Israel;
> for the Lord fighteth for them against the Egyptians.
> (Exodus 14:25)

But it was too late. The waters stood no longer in high walls but swept down over the Egyptians drowning every last one of them including their horses. And the Israelites continued on the other side of the cloud to walk, oblivious to what was happening behind them and the cloud, to the other side of the sea where, when they were safely out of it, they saw the destruction behind them, the bodies of the Egyptians dead upon the sea shores, carriage parts bobbing in the water, no longer viable vehicles for the dead soldiers.

Lord, help me to go through my life well aware that You will not call me to do anything that will not have a perfectly planned end.

> ...and I will get me honour ... And the Egyptians shall
> know that I am the Lord ... (Exodus 14:17-18)

You have everything planned out. You are my great protector. Help me to remember that no matter what trials I face and walk through, there are a million other things that You are keeping me from seeing and knowing are happening around me. There is so much more danger, so many more attacks that You are thwarting that I don't know anything about and probably never will. You protect me from more even during those times when I feel You are allowing me to walk through too much. Help me to understand that everything You do is for Your glory. Help me to realize that You are right there by my side keeping Your cloud of protection around me even when I cannot see it. Help me to trust You completely.

100 – I Want to Hear You

Willow is our sassy, little protégé, a little girl that we have loved and cared for since she was only eighteen months old. Her visits with us are a whirlwind of messes, chaos and questions wrapped up in love, hugs and kisses. As she tags along behind me through the house, she is famous for asking the same questions over and over again. Sometimes, when I am not in the best of moods, I get a bit irritated with being bombarded by the repetition. So, we started asking her a question back. "Willow, do you really need to ask a question that you already know the answer to?" She always, answers with a sweet, "No," and moves on to her next barrage of questions. We have gone over with Willow, that she needs to use her "listening ears" and pay attention using the answers she already knows to obey, keeping her out of trouble. We talked to her so much about needing to use her listening ears, that when we went to visit my friend, Heather at her book store, Willow handed over every set of "bad ears" to *Miss Feather* so that she could try to remember to only use her "good ears" moving forward.

I realized recently that I am guilty of pulling a "Willow" on Jesus. I follow Him around asking Him the same questions repeatedly when He has already answered them clearly a long time ago.

My number one question is, what is my purpose? I try to complicate the Christian life with questions that God has already answered very simply. His purpose is the same for each Christian. We are each given a mission of God the minute we are born again. The simple answer to our purpose is that we are to be God's reflection here on earth. We are to imitate Him and His love and bring others to Him using the particular set of talents that He blessed us with.

> For we are his workmanship, created in Christ Jesus unto good works, which God hath before ordained that we should walk in them. (Ephesians 2:10)

My second favorite repetitive questions is, "Why?!" "Why me?" "Why this?" "Why not?" Why do You allow good people to suffer? Why do You choose to answer one person one way and another in a very different way? Why do You treat similar cases so differently? Why do You allow children to suffer? Why do You allow murder and war to happen? Why do You not give me the answers I want when I want them? And on and on I go.

When we act like we do not understand God's purpose for disease sickness, etc. it is again simply because we have not listened to or do not want to listen to the simple answer, He gave a long, time ago. Everything is *for His glory*. He does not cause the problems but allows them so that the end result can magnify Him. He is not willing that any should perish, but that all should come to repentance. Sometimes, it takes the suffering of an innocent for someone else to be brought to the saving knowledge of Jesus. Sometimes it takes an outsider witnessing the faith that we demonstrate when going through trials for them to place their faith in the Savior.

Jesus does not want us to suffer, but He knows that we will all be healed and whole in heaven, and the things we suffer here on earth are for the advancement of His kingdom and for His glory.

Lord, help me not to frustrate You when I keep asking You the same questions, the ones You have already answered. Help me to slow down and listen. Help me to open my ears and hear what You have already spoken to me. Help me to know that asking the same question repeatedly is not going to change Your answer. Help me to put aside the habit of running my mouth so much that I cannot hear You for my own conversation. Open my ears so that I may hear You.

101 - My Favorite Miracle

> Then took they up stones to cast at him: but Jesus hid himself, and went out of the temple, going through the midst of them, and so passed by. (John 8:59)

Sometimes I find it interesting to take a look at the miracles of Jesus, not just to review His awesome power, but also to find the more subtle pieces of the stories behind the miracles.

One of my favorite miracles is found in John 8:59 and never have I heard it taught in Sunday school ... *Jesus hid Himself, and went out of the temple, going through their midst.*

Many versions of the Bible leave out that line. And it kills me because that line means so much and is so very interesting.

These people were ready to kill Jesus. He had the undivided attention of the whole crowd who had already picked up stones, aiming them at Him with the intent to kill. Yet, He slipped right out, unnoticed.

The Bible clearly states that He walked right through the crowd hidden. Another miracle that Jesus performed, invisibility! He made himself unseen by all those people who were staring right at Him ready to murder Him. But it wasn't God's time for Him to die or the manner in which the prophecy said that He would die. The next verse really gets me.

> As He passed by, He saw a man blind from birth ...(John 9:1)

Another miracle; site to a blind man and only the disciple saw it, and yet the miracle was accomplished right in the midst of that murderous crowd.

The would-be assassins were dumbfounded as we see in verse twelve of chapter nine. They were still looking for Him after His disappearance when this former blind man showed up sighted! They put the newly sighted, blind man through an inquisition. ... "Where is he?" he said, "I do not know."

Jesus had performed the miracle on the blind man, making a mud pack and having a whole conversation with him, sending him off to wash, carrying on a conversation with the disciples, "as He passed by?" That, to me proves He was invisible to whom He wanted to be. How else would no one in that killer crowd have witnessed the miracle?

Maybe it's just me that finds His miracle of invisibility so amazing. But then I find everything He has done amazing.

Lord thank You for being such an awesome God. Thank You for doing the impossible, especially when it comes to my salvation. I am constantly awed and amazed by You. Please continue to open my eyes. Take away the blindness of my carnal nature and help me to see more truths about You every day!

Ali Dixon

102 - His Lavish Love

This morning as I leafed through the pages of my Bible, I saw before my eyes the most picturesque version of the lavish love of God.

> He made him to ride on the high places of the Earth that he might eat the encrease of the fields and suck honey out of the rock and oil out of the flinty rock. (Deuteronomy 32:13)

My mind went for a ride through fields of wheat, ripe for harvest, grains bursting golden from the center of their waving awns. Alongside of the wheat field, jagged rocks jut out of the ground, bees hummed busily around a hive tucked away in a crevice protected from rain wind and creatures by the strength of the rock.

As I allowed my mind to wander, I imagined the wheat being gathered by the harvesters and the grains being ground and made into rich, nourishing bread that would fill the stomach and satisfy hunger. The honey from the rock, taken from the hive near the field, provided not only nutrition when added to the bread, but also sweet delight, joy and pleasure.

As this beautiful picture of the nourishment provided by our Savior passed in front of my eyes, Psalm 81:16 fell open.

> He should have fed them also with the finest of the wheat: and with honey out of the rock should I have satisfied thee. (Psalm 81:16)

Sadness fell over me when I began to feel the disappointment that God must feel when He offers such lavish provisions for us and we turn up our noses at what He has provided so freely. He places bounty before us and we do not listen to His voice, calling us to dine.

O, that my people had hearkened unto to me … (Psalm 81:13)

Lord, help us to eat freely from the lavish provisions You have offered up in Your Word. Help us to nourish our souls through the intake of Your Scripture that offers both the necessary things of life and the joy to top it off.

Help us to drink in the sweetness of Your Word from You, our Rock and our Redeemer. Help me to feed daily on Your Word and help others to see the bounty You have placed before us all. Thank You for providing everything I will ever need.

103 - Face Answers Face

As in water face answereth to face, so the heart of man to man. (Proverbs 27:19)

Yesterday's birthday party resulted in lots of photos and reality slapping me in the face. Seeing myself through the eye of the camera really made me see just how much weight I have put on and how much less attractive I have become over the past few years. That *mirror* image is undeniable and now that I have seen myself as I truly am, I must make a choice. Do I start working out, putting myself through the rigorous routine I once had that made me healthy and strong? Or do I continue the easy path, eating whatever appeals to me and allowing my body to remain plump unhealthy and unappealing?

Just as I examined my physical condition through the photographs and determined that I am on the wrong path and desperately in need of new direction, each of us must take a good, long look at the condition of our heart and our relationship with Jesus. Are we truly exercising our salvation properly? Are we communicating with our Savior daily? Are we on a healthy diet of the Word, or just snacking here and there when it seems convenient allowing ourselves to become fat lazy and ineffective?

Lord, help me to truly examine my heart to make sure that I am walking down the correct path with You, feeding consistently on a steady diet of Your Word. Don't ever let me make excuses for an unhealthy lifestyle of lazily avoiding conversation with You. I want to look at my reflection in the water and see only You.

104 - I Will Joy In the God of My Salvation

Mom and I were discussing some of the negativity found in some of my writing. We discussed how David wrote a lot of negativity but wrapped it up in praise to our Father.

Somehow, we ended up talking about Anne of Green Gables and how Anne had admitted to Marilla that she was in the *depths of despair* Marilla sharply rebuked her reminding Anne that, "To despair is to turn your back on God." Sometimes we need that rebuke, no matter how stinging it may feel in order to get our mind back in the right place, and re-focus on God and His plan rather than our own discomfort and unhappiness with the way things may be going in life.

King David's life was riddled with highs and lows, sorrow and joy, life and death, sin and praise. But through it all, David kept a very personal relationship with God. His conversations where often painful and almost brazen, but always intimate.

This is the kind of relationship that God wants us to have with him. God knows that we are not always going to be upbeat and glowing. But He also doesn't want us to wallow in the negativity of the moment. He wants us to learn from the negative moments, to lament, but also to praise. He wants us to be aware of the negative so that we can repent and learn to joy in Him. He does not want us to turn our backs on Him, to shake our fist in His face and dwell in the depths of despair.

Lord, help me to weigh my own heart to identify what I am feeling, understanding that You already know it all. You understand the pain, joy or passion that I am feeling and want me to verbalize it to You so that I can be aware of my own needs and even more aware when You meet them.

I praise You for knowing me better than I know myself and for putting up with me when I fall into those pits of doubt and fear. I thank You for the forgiveness You have given to me, and I promise to do my best to be worthy of that forgiveness.

Thank You for helping me to hear Your voice. Help me to listen for it always and to continually learn from You and learn to depend on You more and more each day. I am totally amazed by You.

> Although the fig tree shall not blossom, neither shall fruit be in the vines; the labour of the olive shall fail, and the fields shall yield no meat; the flock shall be cut off from the fold, and there shall be no herd in the stalls: Yet I will rejoice in the Lord, I will joy in the God of my salvation. (Habakkuk 3:17-18)

105 - Of Him — Through Him — To Him

Sometimes when I read The Bible, I sort of step out away from reality in into the story that I'm reading.

This morning I was reading in Romans.

> For of Him, and through Him, and to Him, are all things:
> to whom be glory forever. Amen. (Romans 11:36)

"Of Him … through Him … to Him …"

Everything we have been blessed with comes because God allows it. Likewise, everything we wish we had and don't also is a part of our life because God has planned it that way.

Step with me into the story of Job. God allowed Satan to literally torture him. It appears God had completely turned his back on Job. Job had done nothing wrong. He was such a man of faith and he lived his life making sure to do all through and to the Lord.

I cannot imagine the feeling of rejection that Job must have suffered. I personally would have begun to doubt that God loved me or even existed. Job lost everything including his children and his very own health. He was a thoroughly broken man. Yet, he still did everything through God and for God. I know that Job could see no light at the end of the tunnel as even his wife advised him to turn his back on God and die. But he somehow remained faithful and in the end of it all, saw the blessings from God as God replaced and doubled everything he had lost.

But here is where it really gets tough. Everyone Talks about how joyous the return of everything to Job was. But I have never heard mention the struggle he must have gone through for the rest of his life while God worked on those replacements.

Ali Dixon

The rebuilding process took many years and much hard work. He didn't get those ten children he lost back in his arms here on Earth. Yes, he had the comfort of knowing that he would see them again someday in heaven. But he still had to live with the mourning of ten children dead and gone from his arms never to be held again.

And then the ten more that God blessed him with did not just magically appear overnight. The miracle of birth is a long, drawn out process, spread out over time. Each new birth must have brought with it a pang, a tinge of fear that this one might also be taken from him.

As the family grew over the years and developed into adults, I can feel Job's pain each time they all got together for a meal under one roof. The thought must have nagged in the back of his mind, "What if this roof caves in too?" I personally would have insisted on outdoor barbecues under the sky rather than indoor, sit down meals at a table always with a bit of fear in the back of my brain.

But Job was faithful. And through it all he remained faithful. He did not allow the storms of life to destroy him or to destroy his faith in God. He was dug in, grounded, rooted in the knowledge and hope that God would do everything right in His time, in His way, for His purpose. *"Of Him ... through Him ... to Him."*

Lord, let me live with the strength of Job, understanding that although life does not always go the way that we want it to go, You have a reason for everything, a purpose for everything, and in the end all will work out beautifully because it was designed by You. Even if my prayers are not answered until I am with You in glory, I will trust You. I will put all my problems and my sorrows in Your hands. I will do all, acknowledging that everything is of You, through You and for Your glory.

106 - Ready to Pardon

…Thou art a God ready to pardon, gracious and merciful, slow to anger, and of great kindness, and forsook them not. (Nehemiah 9:17)

How many times have I questioned my own worth? How many times in my life have I messed up and turned away? How many times has God extended His mercy to those of us who seem unworthy to be forgiven, washed and brought back into the fold?

God proved his mercy many times over throughout scripture beginning with the Israelites and moving right on down through history to you and me.

…thou art a God, *Ready* to pardon …

How I love the dictionary definition of that word, *ready* when used in this sentence: "fully prepared, easily obtainable; within reach."

No matter how messed up we become, God never turned His back on us. Like the father in the story of the prodigal son, God lets us wander astray. He gives us the free will to choose our path, even if it means bedding down in the pig pins of life.

But He always waits, ready, standing, watching, hoping for the day when we humble ourselves and return to Him, dirt and all, and give ourselves into His loving arms, allowing Him to wash us clean and clothe us, fresh in His robes of righteousness.

Lord, thank You that You are ready to pardon. Thank You for letting me feel that I am enough, not because of anything I have done, but because of who You are!

Ali Dixon

Come unto me all ye that labor and are heavy laden, and I will give you rest. Take my yoke upon you, and learn of me; for I am meek and lowly in heart: and ye shall find rest unto your souls. For my yoke is easy, and my burden is light. (Matthew 11:28-30)

Immediately my mind jumps to the farmer's field, long before the invention of John Deere. I see a farmer out in the fields, reigns laced through his fingers, walking behind his beasts of burden, guiding them gently as they drag the plow share through the earth ripping straight rows of farm-worthy soil, from once furrowed ground.

I can imagine the weight of the yolk and the beating of it against the creatures' shoulders as the plow grabs, sticks, and releases as each clot breaks free. The unsteady yet consistently there, rhythm of the pounding, while pulling the weight of the plow as it digs in and pulls back against the efforts of the beasts, rocking through their bodies vibrating to their very core.

But take another look. Behind the beasts goes the farmer. He is with the beasts every step of the way. His strong arms hold the weight of the plow, so it rides straight and tall and does not allow it to tip to either side. His hands blister and bleed as the handles rub his hands raw as the plow hitting the dirt vibrates up through the beam and through his own body.

All the while the farmer speaks instruction to his beasts, giving them commands, guiding them with the reigns to keep the path straight and even.

The farmer never leaves the field until his beasts of burden do. Then, when plowing is done, the farmer gently leads his beast to rest, shelter and food, washing them clean, removing the caked-on filth of the workday, making them comfortable. But the farmers work is not over when the beasts are bedded down to rest. He still has ahead of him the sowing of the seed, tending of the fields while his harvest grows, and then on to the harvest itself.

Jesus never asks us to take on a burden, a task of any magnitude, and then just walks away. He is there for the long haul *and* the aftermath. He guides us gently while working right alongside of us, and continues to finish the work long after we are cleaned up, made comfortable and bedded down to rest.

Lord, help me to gladly take on whatever tasks that I can do for You. I know that You will not ever asked me to go anywhere that You have not already been. I know that You have planned out the rows, the paths of my life, and will guide me all the way to keep my life straight and useful for Your purpose. Thank You for planning not only the labor, but also the rest. Thank You for teaching, guiding, and more importantly taking on so much of the labor Yourself that it makes my burden light.

Ali Dixon

108 – Breath Life

The day before Thanksgiving, Peggy and I ran to the grocery store to pick up a couple of items that somehow had fallen off my list the last trip.

A while back I made a promise to God to always be aware of the way I present myself in public so I will never turn another human away from God. That being said, when we are out and about it is my habit to smile at *everyone* I meet, no matter who they are or what type of mood they seem to be in.

As we walked past the cheese aisle, we crossed paths with an elderly woman walking in the opposite direction, shopping cart heavily laden with the ingredients for her upcoming Thanksgiving meal. I greeted her with the warm smile and walked on down the aisle past her.

As we passed, she growled under her breath, "don't you dare smile at me when you walk past me." I nearly froze in my tracks, her rebuke totally unexpected. My daughter nearly got whiplash turning to look at the woman, both of us second-guessing our hearing.

> A merry heart doeth good like a medicine: but a broken
> spirit drieth the bones. (Proverbs 17:22)

How sad to lose hope! How sad to be so miserable in your own skin that you can do nothing more than rebuke someone who greets you with love. How sad to be preparing for Thanksgiving when it seems that you are thankful for nothing.

I look around at what we have become as a people. As in Ezekiel's vision, as far as the eye can see, there is nothing but dry bones. Joy has been trampled out of life and there is no value to human dignity any longer. Where is the joyful life that God so desperately wants us to have? He wants each child of His creation to drink of the waters of eternal life, to live in His love. God gave us as Christians two simple Commandments; Love the Lord your God and love your neighbor as yourself.

Reading through the dry bones story in Ezekiel thirty-seven, I noticed something very interesting. When God took Ezekiel out and showed him the valley of the dry bones, God could very well have raised those bones up to life and breathed the breath of life back into them without Ezekiel's help. But God employed him. He commanded Ezekiel to call the dry bones back to life, *"oh ye dry bones, hear the word of the Lord ...."* He told Ezekiel to bid the wind, in His name, to breathe life back into them.

God is asking those of us who love Him and know Him to help breathe life back into the dry bones around us through the spreading of His love, His joy, His Word.

> Jesus said unto him, Thou shalt love the Lord thy God with all thy heart, and with all thy soul, and with all thy mind. This is the first and great commandment. And the second is like unto it, Thou shalt love thy neighbour as thyself. On these two commandments hang all the law and the prophets. (Matthew 22:37-40)

Jesus, help us, through You, to breathe life back into the dry bones around us. It is not always easy. We may be rebuked, laughed at, hated; but You went through so much more pain than that for us. Help us to spread Your love even if it is through a tiny smile that shines a little light into someone's dark day. When we are rebuked for sharing the joy You have placed inside of us, help us to bleed out even more joy.

Let Your Spirit live in me. Help me to maintain the joy that You have given me especially when people try and crush it out. Your joy is my strength.

109 - Having Done All to Stand

Wherefore take unto you the whole armor of God, that ye may be able to withstand in the evil day, and having done all, to stand. (Ephesians 6:13)

Last weekend my daughter and I took the paddle boards out to the lake to enjoy a little bit of mama-daughter time together before she had to go to work.

Standing up on the paddle board is not as easy as people make it look. I stood and got my balance and began to paddle out from the cove towards the open lake. About five minutes into our paddling experience two jet skis went by way out on the middle of the lake.

I thought nothing of it. I kayak all the time on the same lake and the wake from the jet skis and boats does not bother me. I have taken my boat out hundreds of times and never had an issue. But paddle boarding is different. When paddle-boarding, one is standing on an inflated piece of hard, flat rubber on the open water.

Suddenly the wake from the distant jet skis passed under my paddle board as I stood sideways to the wave. I must have looked like a dancing monkey trying to maintain my balance on that board before diving down into the lake. I clung to my paddle and my hat as I surfaced and swam back to the sturdy looking board that floated patiently on the water laughing at me.

I had *done all to stand* as I made an idiot spectacle of myself, grasping at the board and clinging to the air, dancing haphazardly, trying to maintain balance when there was no balance to be had.

I believe this is what God is talking about when He says, *"...and having done all to stand."* Having done all, holding on to something grasping at anything possible to stand, trying to keep your balance, not just succumbing to the waves in life.

I had never seen this passage of scripture this way before. Always before my focus has been on the whole armor of God. This time I realized that it's not just about putting on the armor. It's about holding on and clinging to God, grasping at His Word and absorbing all of it; not being afraid of how we look to other people as we live out our life with purpose to stand for Him no matter what life throws at us or raises up under us trying to tip us.

Lord help me keep my balance. Give me something to cling to. Hold me up right when I cannot stand and keep me from plunging into the waves below me. Let me hold on to You when there is nothing but air to grasp at. You are my life jacket; You are the only one who can pull me up out of the waves when I do fall in. Thank You for rescuing me and being there when I have done all to stand and just can't keep my balance. I love You Jesus. Amen.

Ali Dixon

110 - Choose the Good Stuff

Martha. Martha, thou art careful and troubled about many things: but one thing is needful: and Mary hath chosen that good part which shall not be taken away from her. (Luke 10:41-42)

Over this past little while, I've been down with some big stomach issues. Everyone keeps encouraging me to slow down and let my body heal. But I'm afraid to stop. I've always figured that if I stopped doing, I'll die. And there's too much to get done to do that! So, I keep going ... on and on ...

Now, with the art show coming up on the twenty-eighth of next month, the crochet magazine wanting my patterns professionally tested before agreeing to publish, the book publisher breathing down my neck for me to submit my book proposal, and working a full time job, I don't seem to have enough hours in my day. I try to balance it all so that I can also keep a clean, comfortable home from my family. But somehow, I just can't seem to do all I need to do.

As I rushed through my Bible reading this morning so I could get back to finishing the crochet pattern I am writing, I saw myself in Martha, tattle-telling to Jesus about my own workload and how it isn't fair that "Mary" just leaves it all to me and sits at Jesus' feet while I struggle to get it all done. I felt Jesus reach out to me, lay His gentle hand over mine, look into my eyes and say, "But Mary his chosen the good stuff, Ali." Tears welled up in my eyes.

Lord, forgive me for rushing my time with You to tend to all the other intricacies of my day. I want and need *the good stuff*. Without You constantly by my side I can never get through my day. And without Your blessing, none of what I am working toward will ever be possible.

Help me to make the Martha in me see the importance of sitting with Mary at Your feet and absorbing as much of You as I can. You are the one who blesses me with the time and strength that I do have. You are the author of the opportunities that are coming my way.

Help me to use my time wisely and to understand that the wisest use of my time is to begin my mornings at Your feet completely focused on You, choosing the good stuff.

111 - Epistle of Christ

> ...ye are manifestly declared to be the epistle of Christ ministered by us, written not with ink, but with the Spirit of the living God; not in tables of stone, but in fleshy tables of the heart. (2 Corinthians 3:3)

What does it mean to *be* the epistle of Christ? An epistle is a letter written on paper.

Our Christian testimony is His Word in living breathing flesh. Our lives are probably the only scripture that will ever be read by some people. Therefore, we must be careful that the words spilling off our pages are His Words and not our own. Our author is Christ. If the words pouring out of our pages are not Godly or convey mixed messages, we are a bad example of our author and can confuse and misdirect the reader. As text messages are often misread or misconstrued for lack of punctuation or clarity, so can we cause problems and doubts in the lives of others by allowing our presentation of what He has to say, to be smudged and muddled or hidden under a bushel so that it cannot be read clearly.

A letter is written for clarity not for hidden meanings. Lord do not allow my readers to have to read between the lines and interpret for themselves what Christianity really is. Make my life clarity of Your purpose. Let the epistle written on my heart and pouring out through my daily life be Your words clear and true and precise.

112 - Thy Face, Lord, Will I Seek

When thou saidst, Seek ye my face; my heart said unto thee, Thy face, Lord, will I seek. (Psalms 27:8)

Seeking God's face isn't just about reading His word and looking for Him on the passages written there. Seeking Jesus is about being aware of Him every minute of every day. Looking for His touch in all that we experience.

It is easy to recognize His hand when we walk out in nature. When we step away from the hustle and bustle of the city and into the glorious woods, or walk by a stream, we are so close to Him. His voice whispering through the leaves as they are caught in the breeze, or His laugh in the gurgling stream, can almost be heard, sending shivers of excitement through us as we experience His presence firsthand.

It is harder to seek His face when we are surrounded by the mundane, ordinary aspects of life. As we sit at our desks, running numbers for forty hours a week, His voice can seem silent and we only hear the keyboards clattering around us. Phones ring. Customers can be irrational, and our lives can feel so empty. It is during these times that we truly need to seek His face. Times when it is the hardest to find Him are times when we need Him the most.

Lord, I want to seek You. I want to know You. I want to feel Your presence in every aspect of my life. Show Your face to me every day in everything I do. Amen.

Ali Dixon

113 - No Fear in Love

As a few of you know, I came from out of ten years in an extremely abusive relationship. And because of this I have developed some very strange habits. I live my entire life trying to please others, trying to do more, never being able to rest or relax because, for so many years, the moment I stopped doing, everything broke loose.

I'm tough as nails when it comes to physical labor or pain inflicted. I'm not afraid of spiders, scorpions and other bugs. I hike alone in the woods where I know the Bears live with no fear.

But when a human raises their voice or hand at me, I tend to freeze. I can almost literally feel the ice crystals crawl up through my veins, hardening my heart towards the individual inflicting the pain, preparing me for the blows, whether emotional or physical.

Rather than lashing out in anger, tears tend to well up in my eyes. I walk away to avoid being hurt rather than allowing for more pain. When someone asks me to make even a simple decision, I am almost immobilized ... "If I say I want to eat at a certain restaurant, am I choosing wrong? What if the other person wanted something other than what I want?" Making the wrong decision scares me to death as silly as it may seem.

When I came home to Jesus it was really difficult for me to accept His forgiveness because I knew all the errors I have made in my life, and I knew that He knew them just as well if not better than I. It was hard for me to grasp the concept that I do not have to perform well for Jesus to love me. I had to really learn to grasp the fact that He loves me no matter what.

> There is no fear in love; but perfect love casteth out fear: because fear hath torment. He that feareth is not made perfect in love. (1 John 4:18)

Thank You, Lord, for helping me to grasp the concept that, no matter what mistakes, no matter how many poor decisions I have made, nothing I could ever do will separate me from Your love. I trust You completely. Please keep working on me to get over the fears I have towards humanity. Help me to learn that I don't have to seek approval to be loved unconditionally. Please take away the anxiety that lives inside of me daily, anxiety that brings me to my knees causing me to seek the approval of others. I want to live my life to be worthy of Your love, and Your love alone, and not worry so much about what everyone else thinks of me.

Ali Dixon

114 - Living God

Forasmuch then as we are the offspring of God, we ought
not to think that the Godhead is like unto gold, or silver,
or stone, graven by art and man's device. (Acts 17:29)

Often, I believe that Christians do not understand the concept of a true
relationship with God. We confine Him to, *temples made with hands* and
worship as idol worshipers, following rituals and routines of worship as
those who bow to images created by the hands of men.

But my God is not a carved image, sitting on a pedestal, created by
man. My God is alive and active and powerful and as such deserves a
worship to match who He truly is! His Word is not just print on a page,
but alive and moving on a daily basis. This concept excites me! It makes
me want to search for Him in all of creation, in all my everyday activities.

Lord help me to think on You and be aware of Your presence every
single day of my life, every single minute of my being. Help me to align
my heart and my soul and my mind with You so that I feel Your living
spirit within me all the time. Help me to worship You as the living God
that You are. Don't ever let me treat You as an idol carved by the hands
of men sitting on a pedestal with no power to move of itself. You are an
awesome, living God! And I praise You for who You are!

115 - Your Mercies are New Each Morning

For many years I lived in fear of my Creator. I saw God as a threat, a punisher. I felt anxiety when I consider all the ways I had fallen away from the rules that have been laid out before me as a child. I knew I deserved the wrath of vengeful God. After all, I had willfully turned my back on Him and run as far from Him and anything having to do with Him as was humanly possible.

But then I found the "God" meaning of fear. The kind of fear that God wants from us is not the shake in my boots kind of fear, but reverence, awe and amazement for all He is an all He does for us.

We are to fear Him as a child fears the good, good father who loves with all his heart, yet disciplines to keep the child on the right path so that he may grow into a good, responsible adult.

> The Lord taketh pleasure in them that fear him, in those
> that hope in his mercy. (Psalm 147:11)

It is spelled out clearly. Fear is equivalent to awe for His mercy, hope in His loving kindness.

Fear is a reverence, an awe over the steadfast love that He offered up for us so freely when Jesus came and died on the cruel cross for our sins so that we no longer must fear eternal damnation in hell. Fear, as we humanly know it, is replaced by love.

Thank You, Jesus, for what You did for me on the cross. Thank You for taking my fears and burying them in hell. Thank You for replacing them with Your steadfast love. I so love You and adore You. I hope in Your loving kindness. Your mercies are new to me each morning.

Ali Dixon

Conclusion

Never have I seen myself the way I did today. The laugh lines (as momma called them) around my eyes and mouth, the fading freckles on my paling skin ... all flaws that have been pointed out to me over and over ... But none of it bothered me this time. I saw instead a happy woman, one who has not emerged in years. I saw eyes that sparkled with joy instead of being drowned in sadness and disappointment with life in general. I almost saw the girl I once was before I let myself follow the path that I designed instead of the one laid out for me by God. I saw a woman who had been deeply scarred emotionally and physically, healed by forgiveness, acceptance and love. I saw before me all the imperfections that God has made perfect by His grace. I saw His daughter, a princess, perfect by His design ... not perfect in beauty, but perfect in love ...

> For we ourselves also were sometimes foolish, disobedient, deceived, serving divers lusts and pleasures, living in malice and envy, hateful, and hating one another. BUT AFTER THAT the kindness and love of God our Saviour toward man appeared, Not by works of righteousness which we have done, but according to his mercy he saved us, by the washing of regeneration, and renewing of the Holy Ghost; (Titus 3:3-5)

About The Author

Ali was raised as a missionary kid on the border of Texas and Mexico. She spent four of her younger years living in southern Mexico in the city of Oaxaca where she became fluent in Spanish, and in the Word of God.

After high-school, Ali abandoned all that she had been taught by her parents and mentors throughout the years and struck out on her own to make herself into the worldly creature that she somehow thought she ought to be.

Many hard years later, a broken Ali returned home to Jesus and was welcomed back with open arms. Her new-found love for Him created a passion inside that could not be contained.

It is her desire to share the love she found with as many as will open their ears and listen to what she has learned and what Jesus has to offer in the pages of this book and through her Facebook blog, *Coffee With Jesus*.

Printed in the United States
By Bookmasters